About the Authors

PATT LEVINE is a professional writer who has been a serious cook for many years. In addition to her long career in advertising as an executive-level copywriter for both retail stores and advertising agencies, she has had recipes published in *Gourmet* magazine. After battling weight problems since her early thirties, she decided to have weight reduction surgery in April 2003. Realizing that she would have to drastically change her way of cooking and eating after surgery, she developed a high-protein, low-fat food program that includes everything from soup to dessert. Working with her coauthor, Michele Bontempo-Saray, Patt has combined her two areas of expertise in this cookbook to help other people who have had, or are thinking of having, weight reduction surgery to achieve their weight loss goals while enjoying delicious food. Patt graduated from the Fashion Institute of Technology in New York City with a degree in communications. In addition to writing, she designs most of her own clothes, has been a professional singer, and has taught advertising copywriting at two New York colleges. Patt lives in New York City with her husband, Bob, and Ossie cat, Mischa.

MICHELE BONTEMPO-SARAY is an art director and graphic designer who has worked in both the fashion and home furnishing fields. Her career has included positions in some of New York's top department stores as well as a number of advertising, design, and catalog agencies. She and her business partner, Richard Oreiro, also ran their own advertising catalog and design agency for ten years. Known for her innate sense of "what looks right," Michele has also been involved in a number of corporate identification and interior design projects. Michele was born in London, England, and grew up in the Bronx, New York. She has also lived in Italy and Canada. She and her husband, Michael, live in New York City.

Eating Well after
Weight Loss Surgery

Patt Levine and Michele Bontempo-Saray

Foreword by WILLIAM B. INABNET, MD, FACS
Consulting Nutritionist, MEREDITH URBAN-SKURO, MS, RD

Eating Well after
WEIGHT LOSS
Surgery

Over 140 Delicious Low-Fat,

High-Protein Recipes to

Enjoy in the Weeks, Months

and Years after Surgery

MARLOWE & COMPANY
NEW YORK

EATING WELL AFTER WEIGHT LOSS SURGERY:
*Over 140 Delicious Low-Fat, High-Protein Recipes to Enjoy
in the Weeks, Months, and Years after Surgery*

Published by
Marlowe & Company
An Imprint of Avalon Publishing Group Incorporated
245 West 17th Street • 11th floor
New York, NY 10011

AVALON
publishing group incorporated

Library of Congress Cataloging-in-Publication Data
Levine, Patt.—Eating well after weight loss surgery: Over 140 low-fat,
high-protein recipes to enjoy in the weeks, months and years after sur-
gery/Patt Levine and Michele Bontempo-Saray; foreword by
William B. Inabet; consulting nutritionist, Meredith Urban-Skuros.
p. cm.
Includes index.
ISBN 1-56924-453-7
1. Obesity—Surgery—Popular works. 2. Weight loss—Popular works. 3. Eating—Popular works.
I. Bontempo-Saray, Michelle. II. Title.

RD540.L465 2004
641.5'635—dc22   2004040327

9 8

Designed by Pauline Neuwirth, Neuwirth and Associates, Inc.

Printed in the United States of America
Distributed by Publishers Group West

Contents

Foreword

by William B. Inabnet

$\mathcal{O}$BESITY IS AN epidemic of unprecedented proportions that is rapidly becoming one of the greatest health risks of our time. It is now estimated that 65 percent of American adults are overweight, with 15 percent being more than 100 pounds over their ideal body weight. The health and socioeconomic implications of obesity are enormous. The incidence of associated medical problems, such as diabetes, hypertension, sleep apnea, gastrointestinal esophageal reflux disease, arthritis, and depression, is greatly increased in obese individuals. These problems not only decrease life expectancy but also place a heavy burden on our health care system, which is already experiencing a tremendous strain. Obesity can lower self-esteem, leading to a vicious cycle of overeating and increased weight gain. Workplace and societal discrimination can also greatly exacerbate the problem.

In order to understand the available mechanisms for weight loss, it is important to have an understanding of how the body regulates eating. The human body is a complex biological system that requires essential nutrients to function normally. Vitamins, minerals, glucose, and protein are all necessary for the body to maintain itself in a healthy state. The intake of these key nutrients is greatly influenced by eating behavior, which itself is influenced by numerous biological and environmental factors. Eating behavior is regulated by the body's hunger center, which is located in the hypothalamus of the brain. In response to the ingestion of food, the gastrointestinal tract releases a variety of hormones (substances that are released by one tissue and travel through the bloodstream to act on another distant tissue) that act directly on the hunger center to decrease appetite. During periods of fasting, these gastrointestinal hormone levels are elevated, thereby causing a sense of hunger. Environmental factors that influence eating behavior include the increased availability of fast food, junk food, and larger portion sizes, as well as an increasingly sedentary lifestyle in the era of computers and wide-screen televisions.

In most people, weight gain can be explained by a simple formula: when energy intake exceeds energy expenditure, the body gains weight. In simpler terms, if you ingest more calories and nutrients than your body requires, you will gain weight.

Weight loss can be achieved by decreasing intake (i.e., dieting), increasing activity (i.e., exercise), or both. Dieting and exercise are the preferred methods for weight loss; however, these methods often do not result in sustained long-term weight loss.

When conservative methods of weight loss have been exhausted, certain people may benefit from weight loss surgery. In order to qualify for weight loss surgery, you must be at least 100 pounds over your ideal body weight or 75 pounds over your ideal body weight in the presence of obesity-related medical problems (diabetes, hypertension, sleep apnea, asthma, etc.). Weight loss surgery should be viewed as the beginning of a major lifestyle change that requires a lifelong commitment to leading a healthier life. Healthy eating habits, exercise, and nutritional diligence are all important in optimizing weight loss following surgery. Since your intake is restricted and the amount of nutrients that you absorb is decreased, you will need to take daily vitamin supplements for the rest of your life, including iron, calcium, and a multivitamin.

Three weight-loss operations are performed to induce weight loss—adjustable gastric banding, gastric bypass, and biliopancreatic diversion with duodenal switch. No one procedure is superior to another, as each operation has advantages and disadvantages. Many factors go into recommending a particular weight loss procedure, such as your weight, age, eating habits, presence of obesity-related medical problems, and surgery preference. Adjustable gastric banding is performed by placing a silicone band around the inlet of the stomach, thereby creating a small upper portion and a larger lower portion of the stomach. The band is connected to a small tube and reservoir that allows your surgeon to adjust the diameter of the band by making it tighter or looser depending on your degree of restriction. Adjustments are typically performed in your surgeon's office in a matter of minutes. The key to successful weight loss is to find the optimal diameter that allows you to have sufficient restriction to lose weight, but not so much that vomiting is induced. Patients often report a feeling of satiety much earlier in the eating process.

Gastric bypass is the most common weight loss operation performed in the United States. With this procedure, the stomach is completely divided, thereby creating a small gastric pouch that is completely separated from the remainder of the stomach. Further downstream, the small bowel is divided and connected to the small gastric pouch, a maneuver that creates a food channel and a digestive juice channel. These two channels meet downstream to re-establish intestinal continuity. Gastric bypass causes you to lose weight by decreasing the amount of food intake and by causing you to absorb fewer calories (and nutrients). If you eat foods rich in sweets, you may experience a condition called dumping, which is characterized by bloating, nausea, and abdominal pain. Gastric bypass patients report a decreased desire for food and get full much earlier in the eating process.

The biliopancreatic diversion with duodenal switch is the most radical of the three weight loss procedures. With this procedure, approximately 75 percent of the stomach is removed so that your stomach is shaped like a banana. The sphincter outlet muscle of the stomach, which is called the pylorus, is preserved, thereby minimizing the chance of dumping. As with gastric bypass, two channels are created, one for food and the other for the digestive juices. But unlike gastric bypass, these channels are much longer and are reconnected further downstream. With this procedure, weight loss is caused primarily by malabsorption with a small amount of restriction. Because the stomach is larger, patients can eat larger portion sizes and sample a greater diversity of food groups than patients who have undergone adjustable gastric banding or gastric bypass. Because of the malabsorption, long-term nutritional deficiencies can occur, especially if patients are not compliant with their nutritional supplements.

Weight-loss surgery is an excellent method of losing weight for individuals who have failed to do so with conservative methods of weight loss, but healthy eating habits and a high motivation are critical to a good outcome. The recipes in this book will help individuals who have undergone weight loss surgery monitor their nutritional intake and serve as a guide for maintaining a healthy eating lifestyle. In people who have not undergone weight loss surgery, this cookbook may prove to be helpful in your struggle to maintain or achieve an ideal body weight. The recipes have been written to make eating an enjoyable but healthy experience. I wish you much success in your journey to lose weight.

WILLIAM B. INABNET, MD, FACS, is Chief of Endocrine Surgery at the College of Physicians and Surgeons of Columbia University in New York and a renowned specialist in bariatric surgery. Dr. Inabnet has written and published extensively and is the author of *Minimally Invasive Endocrine Surgery* (2002) and *Laproscopic Bariatric Surgery*, which is scheduled to be published in September 2004.

Introduction

▷ THE WEIGHT WARS

I WAS NOT always fat. In fact, I was a skinny kid. Then, in my teens and early twenties, I became curvaceous and sexy. But once I started working, I started gaining—a couple of pounds here, a couple of pounds there. So I tried diet pills. They worked for a while, but I was so manic and bitchy while taking them, no one could stand me. When I went off them, I gained all my weight back, plus some. Then I tried dieting. You know, grapefruit, broiled steak, and salad and I never, never ate more than the guys I was dating (one of the golden oldie definitions of "being a lady"). Then I met my husband, a great guy with a great appetite. Any amount that I ate was less than he could put away. So I started gaining and gaining and gaining. I tried Weight Watchers, lost forty pounds, hit a plateau, and gained it all back and then some. I tried going to the gym. That certainly helped, but once my career started taking off and I was working nights, and weekends, and traveling constantly, exercise became erratic, then nonexistent. So I gained. Then I tried the Atkins diet, which was perfect for me because I'm a real carnivore. The first time I tried it, I tested purple all the time (that means that I successfully put myself into ketosis, which is the goal), but I barely lost anything. Then I gained. I tried Atkins again. This time I lost forty pounds, hit a plateau, and gained it all back plus some. Sound familiar?

Over a period of about twenty years, I had more than doubled my weight. I weighed over 300 pounds. I could barely walk a block without stopping to rest. I couldn't fit in theater or airplane seats. I actually broke furniture. After a bout with pneumonia, which landed me in the hospital for over a week, my primary care physician suggested that I consider weight reduction surgery. My pulmonologist concurred. So I did research, talked to a number of people who had undergone the surgery, and decided to do it.

My doctor referred me to Dr. Inabnet, a thoroughly professional and truly compassionate man. He and his staff seemed to understand exactly what I was going through and how I had gotten to this point, without being judgmental. We decided that I was a good candidate for laparoscopic Lap-Band bariatric surgery. The surgery was successful, but then the real battle began. As Dr. Inabnet and his staff reminded me, the surgery is only a tool. Now I had to rethink not only the amount that I ate, but the kinds of foods that I ate and, oh, yeah, start exercising.

Cooking has always been one of my greatest passions—I think I started cooking when I was eight years old. And once I discovered that cooking for other people brought me unconditional approval, well, let's just say that it became a defining part of my persona. Whereas cooking had once played a major role in my weight gain, now I was determined that it would be a significant factor in my weight loss. You see, I love a challenge in the kitchen. For years, I had whipped up gourmet dishes around other people's likes and dislikes, allergies and restrictions. Now, I would put that talent to work for me.

I developed a high-protein, low-fat eating plan with virtually no "bad" carbohydrates. I allowed myself only "good" carbs from fruit and vegetables. The hard part was dealing with the restrictions for the first four months after surgery (but more about that later). Did it work? The answer is yes, although it's still a work in progress. I have lost a significant amount of weight, and I'm looking and feeling pretty terrific, if I do say so myself. I've even started wearing clothes that I haven't been able to get into for years. And what's amazing is that, because of my ongoing weight loss adventure, I wrote this cookbook. Now I can help other people on their road to weight loss in the weeks, months, and years after surgery.

▷ DEPRIVE MYSELF? NOT ME

LET'S FACE IT, one of the reasons most people become candidates for bariatric surgery is that we love to eat. As a self-described "foodie," I admit that I was worried when my nutritionist, Meredith Urban-Skuro, told me about the very restrictive way I would have to eat in the first months after surgery—low-fat food, pureed to the consistency of mush or chopped up in tiny bits. The suggested menus she showed me looked like a hospital soft diet—totally tasteless mush. When I was being kind, I referred to it as baby food. When I was being cynical, I called it sludge.

But just because a food's texture is bland, that doesn't mean its taste has to be. So I set out to see if I could cook low-fat dishes tasty enough to stand up to pureeing or mincing, recipes that not only pleased, but also excited, my palate. As an added complication, I needed to cook for my husband at the same time.

My best friend, Michele, curious about the post-op restrictions on my diet, asked to taste some of the recipes I had developed. She immediately challenged me to write a cookbook for other bariatric surgery patients and offered to help.

This cookbook is proof that you can cook delicious food that not only satisfies your post-surgical guidelines, but also satisfies your taste buds. Yes, there is added work if you are cooking for others as well as yourself, but we've tried to keep it to a minimum. You can use these recipes the way they are written, or use them as a basis for experimenting to create new ones that suit your personal taste.

When I told Meredith and my surgeon, Dr. Inabnet, that I was writing a cookbook for weight reduction surgery patients, they were really excited.

But Meredith warned me. "Patt, I know that you are a very sophisticated cook, but not everyone who is going to use this cookbook will be, so don't make it too complicated or esoteric."

I said, "C'mon, get serious, people who aren't into cooking won't start cooking just because they had the surgery."

That's when Meredith told me something that surprised me. She and Dr. Inabnet found that many of their patients had discovered that unless they had control over what they ate, they ran into some problems; for instance, they ate too much because they couldn't control portion sizes; they didn't know how the food was prepared so they ate unexpected fats, sugars, and other ingredients that created digestive distress. For these reasons, many of those patients *were* starting to cook seriously for the first time after surgery.

So whether you have always been cooking or you are just starting to cook for the first time, I promise that you will enjoy using this cookbook. It will show you how to make delicious, satisfying food that will help you achieve and maintain your weight loss goals over a long period of time.

▷ ABOUT THIS BOOK: YOU *CAN* TURN MUSH INTO MAGIC

LET'S BE HONEST, not everything purees well. I admit it; we had a couple of real disasters while we were developing and testing these recipes. The nice thing about this cookbook is that it progresses along with your eating program—these dishes taste terrific whether they're pureed, chopped up, or served as solid food.

Our cookbook runs the gamut from breakfast and brunch dishes to soups, entrées, and vegetables. Plus, you'll find an entire section on sauces that includes both savory and sweet toppings. And speaking of sweets, we've come up with a number of sweet indulgences that are completely allowable as well as incredibly luscious.

These recipes are high in protein, contain no added sugars, are low in fat, and only contain complex carbohydrates from fruits and vegetables. Therefore, they are protein-rich, low-calorie, and have virtually no "bad carbs." What they do have is enough flavor and variety to keep you from feeling deprived.

Because this cookbook is a collaborative effort, it offers a huge amount of variety. You see, Michele and I have very different tastes in cooking and eating. She likes spicy stuff, like curries and hot peppers. I like fruit and meat combinations and subtle seasonings.

But we both agree on using high-quality ingredients. By developing these recipes together, we came up with many truly original and delectable new dishes.

We offer a wide range of recipes in each category. You'll find variations on classic French and Italian cuisine, exotic Indian and Caribbean dishes, and recipes with Asian and Mexican influences, as well as good old American comfort food. While many of our recipes are quick and uncomplicated, some require longer cooking times or specialized steps—those are the ones that I call "Sunday cooking"—you know, the foods you cook when you have more time, which taste even better reheated the second day. You'll be amazed at how we created some of the richest-tasting dishes without lots of fat or calories. Better than that, we came up with a luscious substitute for mashed potatoes that's so good even meat-and-potato guys love it.

Most of our recipes are designed to serve four people, so if you're cooking for others, they can enjoy the same foods as you're eating. Of course, you'll be eating such a small amount that there may be leftovers. (Why not puree them and reheat them for lunch the next day?)

At the bottom of each recipe you'll find preparation and serving instructions for you to follow at each post-op stage, whether you've had a Lap-Band, gastric bypass, or biliopancreatic diversion with duodenal switch (BPD-DS) procedure. In addition, you'll find portion-size suggestions to help you cook for people who aren't eating a limited diet.

Because these recipes are so delicious and interesting, we think that you and your family are going to enjoy this cookbook for years and years, even after you come to the end of your post-surgical food restrictions.

▷ THE ROAD TO SUCCESS

NEEDLESS TO SAY, your weight loss journey will be unique to you, and it will depend on a number of factors. Once again, as my doctor always reminds me, the surgery is only a tool. Changing your eating and exercise habits are equally important. While we can't do anything to help you burn those calories, we can give you a new way to cook and eat. You won't feel deprived, because it's absolutely delicious. And since it doesn't restrict you to just a few limited types of food, it's easy and healthy enough to follow for a long time, even the rest of your life.

Since I had my surgery, I've experienced a steady weight loss that has made me very happy. The biggest surprise was my husband (our primary guinea pig), who did not have the surgery. By going on a modified version of this eating plan (eating these recipes for breakfast and dinner), he has lost a total of forty-five pounds and has maintained his weight loss ever since. He's living proof that this cookbook works for *anyone* who needs to lose weight.

I am very happy that I decided to have bariatric surgery and I find that almost every day I reach a new, small goal. My life, which had become so restrictive due to my weight, is now full of new possibilities. It's wonderful to once more be able to do the things I used to take for granted when I was slimmer.

Michele and I hope that this cookbook will help you find all the success that you wish for and that you will enjoy every meal that you prepare from this cookbook along the way.

Advice from a Nutritionist

by Meredith Urban-Skuro

*W*HO SAYS IT has to be difficult to find food to eat after weight loss surgery? It may be a little challenging in the beginning, but eventually you will be able to eat almost everything in moderation. And I think that this cookbook can definitely help. There are specific guidelines that need to be adhered to after surgery:

▶ For the first three to four weeks, a pureed, blended diet is recommended for Lap-Band and gastric bypass patients to lessen the chances of an obstruction caused by large particles of food. Obstructions can cause discomfort and may lead to vomiting. The biliopancreatic diversion duodenal switch (BPD-DS) patient can usually tolerate a soft, mushy consistency for the first three weeks. Advancing to solid foods can usually occur between two to six weeks after surgery. This book features very specific week-by-week preparation and portion-size guidelines at the bottom of each recipe, which can help you manage your diet progression. Check with your doctor or nutritionist on how to advance your diet.

▶ Chewing is key! Relax, enjoy, and taste the food that you are consuming. I encourage all my patients to chew at least *twenty-five times*. Solid food should be cut to the size of a fifth of a fingernail or smaller. If you eat too fast, don't chew your food well, or try to progress to solid food too quickly, you may overfill and vomit.

▶ Mealtime should take no more than thirty minutes. I recommend three meals and one to two healthy snacks during the day. Remember to measure and weigh your food so you are aware of the portion size you are eating.

▶ The nutritional emphasis in this cookbook is on protein foods. However, we do encourage a variety of foods and well-balanced meals. A strong emphasis needs to be placed on choosing high-protein foods. Protein is essential for growth, repair, and formation of new tissue. Protein aids in wound healing, maintains lean body mass, is a source of energy, and helps prevent protein malnutrition.

▶ Great protein choices are meat, fish, poultry, eggs, cheese, milk, yogurt, beans, and nuts. Solid, dense, protein-rich foods allow you to feel satiated for a longer period of time. Make sure to choose lean cuts of meat, trim off the fat, and take the skin off the poultry to reduce your fat intake.

▶ After weight loss surgery, protein needs vary depending on the type of surgery you have undergone. After the Lap-Band, aim for 50 to 60 grams of protein per day. After a gastric bypass, aim for 50 to 70 grams of protein per day. After a BPD-DS, aim for 80 to 120 grams of protein a day. Not meeting your protein needs can lead to protein malnutrition—a condition that can cause fatigue, weakness, and swelling of lower extremities, as well as hair loss.

▶ I encourage my patients to consume enough liquids between their meals to satisfy their thirst and prevent dehydration. Six to eight 8-ounce glasses of noncaloric, decaffeinated liquids are recommended per day. But do not drink immediately before, during, or after meals. Separation of liquids and solids is recommended to maintain a feeling of fullness. Since liquids empty faster from the gastric pouch than solid food, if you drink while you are eating it can dissolve the food and leave you feeling empty, which can cause overeating.

I hope that you will enjoy the fabulous recipes in this unique and exciting cookbook designed especially for you. The more you use it, the closer you'll come to knowing that you cannot only eat right, but also eat well, as you strive to attain your weight loss goals.

MEREDITH URBAN-SKURO, MS, RD, is the Program Coordinator for the Obesity Center at the New York Presbyterian Hospital at Columbia University in New York City. She works closely with the hospital's bariatric surgery unit, providing expert assessment and education to patients both before and after surgery. Meredith has delivered lectures on her specialties—nutrition and bariatric surgery—at professional health care conferences and meetings around the world.

How to Use This Cookbook

$\mathcal{A}$T THE BOTTOM of each recipe, you'll find specific guidelines for preparation and a recommended serving size for every stage of the eating programs for Lap-Band, gastric bypass, and BPD-DS patients. We have also included preparation and serving suggestions for everyone else (referred to as "others"—people who have not had weight reduction surgery). These guidelines are listed under the following headings: *Lap-Band, Bypass, BPD-DS*, and *Others*.

In addition, you'll find a nutritional analysis breakdown below the guideline information. It includes calories, protein, fat, carbohydrates, cholesterol, fiber, and sodium. All analyses are based on an average portion size (*Others'* portions). Obviously, if you are a post-surgical patient, for the first few months you'll be eating smaller portions than the analyzed amounts, so you will be taking in even fewer calories, and less fat, carbs, cholesterol, fiber, and sodium per recipe. (*Note: We rarely add salt while we're cooking; that's why most recipes list "Salt and pepper to taste." Be aware that the salt and pepper you add will not be reflected in the nutritional analyses.*)

You have probably discussed a food program with your doctor and nutritionist. The guidelines we are using were suggested by my nutritionist. Of course, she stressed that people's tolerances vary greatly; so while we may recommend an ingredient or a recipe as being appropriate for a specific stage of your diet progression, only you will know what foods you can tolerate and when you can best tolerate them.

This book is based on my eating adventures and experiences after my Lap-Band surgery. I was very lucky and had almost no digestion problems from the get-go. In fact, I found that I had fewer problems after surgery than I had had before. But I realize that's not always the case. Some people are very sensitive to specific foods after bariatric surgery. If that's the case for you, you may want to delay trying certain recipes until later in your eating program.

For example, if you find that you are unable to comfortably digest something like beef until Week 12 or 16 but you love our recipe, which says you can eat it after Week 8, try preparing the recipe with chicken, turkey, or fish instead. You'll notice that, because many people have problems with gas or bloating from certain vegetables, we don't recommend recipes that include them until Week 8. But, if you're like me, you can eat virtually all vegetables from the very beginning.

Don't be afraid to be flexible. Try adding new foods gradually. This book is all about making the program work for you.

Hints for Food Preparation, Cooking, and Eating

▷ SUGGESTED KITCHEN EQUIPMENT

You will need the following:

A food processor and/or a blender
A mini-processor and/or a mini-chopper
Nonstick cookware
8 4-ounce ramekins
A 4-quart Dutch oven or soup pot

A microwave oven is a real convenience, as it allows you to cook in larger quantities, puree or blend, store in the refrigerator or freezer, and then reheat.

▷ TIPS FOR COOKING

Here are some things that I have discovered through my cooking experiences that may help you:

▶ Spices, herbs, garlic, hot sauce, and mustard have almost no calories and they can make all the difference between being miserable and being satisfied. Don't be afraid to add curry powder to yogurt as a base to puree chicken. Garlic (and we use a lot of it) can liven up just about anything.

▶ When a recipe calls for artificial sweetener, do not use aspartame (Equal or NutraSweet) if you're cooking or baking—aspartame breaks down when heated. Use Splenda or Sweet 'N Low. You can use aspartame for non-cooked dishes.

▶ As someone who used to cook with lots of butter and olive oil, I was amazed that switching to cooking sprays didn't really change the taste of my favorite dishes. But I did find that the flavor of the cooking sprays does often make a difference. That's why in most recipes I specify which cooking spray to use— butter-flavored, olive oil, or canola oil.

▶ In those rare recipes in which butter or margarine is necessary, I use light margarines. Here's a hint: even though the manufacturers of Benecol margarine and other "heart-healthy" lighter margarines (which have half the calories of butter or regular margarine) recommend that they not be used for cooking, you can use them for quick sautéing, like making eggs.

▶ Most cooks have their own personal favorite ingredient. In my case, I cannot cook without some brand of concentrated chicken or beef broth (such as Bovril, Knorr, and Campbell's). I don't mix it with water. I add a teaspoon or two straight from the jar to recipes for maximum flavor.

▶ When a recipe calls for eggs, I generally use an egg substitute (such as Egg Beaters or Better 'n Eggs). When I need whipped egg whites, I usually use egg-substitute whites (like All Whites). But in a few instances, for example, when I make flans or custardlike dishes, I do find that only whole large eggs or whole egg yolks will work. By the way, egg substitutes are pasteurized, so using them in uncooked recipes is not a health hazard.

▶ When a recipe calls for fresh lemon or lime juice, heat the fruit in the microwave on HIGH for 10 seconds. It makes it easier to juice.

▶ Why reinvent the wheel? Commercially-prepared brands of fat-free, sugar-free ice cream, sherbet, and frozen yogurt are as good, if not better, than any that we could devise (and we tried). Of course, they taste terrific when you top them or layer them with one of our dessert sauces. But be careful: many of these diet desserts are made with sugar alcohols (sorbitol and manitol, for example), which can cause gas, diarrhea, and bloating.

▶ I've found that freezing and storing excess food in ice cube trays lets me easily defrost and reheat small portions later on.

▷ TIPS FOR EATING

▶ Here's a hint that's really worked for me: since you can only eat a small amount at each meal, use a salad plate instead of a dinner plate, and a salad fork and teaspoon instead of a dinner fork and soup spoon. You may also want to invest in some small dessert-sized bowls, which are perfect for soups and purees.

▶ If you need to slow down your eating, try using chopsticks—and remember to chew each mouthful twenty-five times (Meredith made me write that).

▶ When eating with others who can have regular-sized portions, try to pace yourself to match the other person so that you don't finish eating before he or she does.

▷ TIPS FOR DRINKING

▶ At my first meeting with my nutritionist, she stressed how important it was that I learn to eat without drinking any liquids immediately before, after, or during my meals. This was one of the toughest things for me to do, as I was the type of person who would tell the waiter at a restaurant to just leave the water pitcher on the table.

▶ I assumed that she stressed this "no drinking rule" because my food capacity was so diminished she did not want me to fill up on liquids. Wrong! She explained that drinking liquids with meals makes the food wash down more easily, so you may actually end up eating more than you should. Obviously, this will defeat the purpose of your surgery.

▶ But even though you can't drink liquids with meals, you do need to drink at least six to eight 8-ounce glasses of water or other noncaloric liquid each day. I keep a glass of diet iced tea or a bottle of water within grabbing distance at all times (except mealtimes, of course).

▷ GENERAL TIPS FOR JUST GETTING ALONG

▶ Since the first few months of soft food allows you no opportunity for chewing, try chewing sugar-free gum. Before I took this advice (offered by my brother-in-law), I found myself clenching and grinding my teeth. Even if you are not a gum-chewer (and I wasn't), keep it handy and chew a piece when no one else is around. Meredith disagrees with this so I'm including her warning: *chewing gum can cause lots of gas.*

▶ Here's an interesting personal discovery I made that may help you, too: Meredith had warned me that after surgery I might have problems with constipation. She suggested that I take a daily fiber supplement, like Citrucel, and I found that sometimes it worked and sometimes it didn't. Then I had an idea: instead of fiber (after all, I was getting plenty of fiber from fruits and vegetables), what if I took one 400 IU softgel of vitamin E everyday? I don't know if it was the vitamin E itself or the tiny amount of soybean oil it was suspended in that was the magic ingredient—but it worked!

Stocking Your Pantry and Refrigerator

*I*F YOU'RE LIKE me, you get really annoyed when you want to make a certain recipe, only to find that you're missing one ingredient. That's why I thought it would be really handy to provide you with a pantry list of the basic essentials, plus some of the specialty ingredients that we used to create these recipes.

I found that having a variety of flavors to choose from made it easier to stick to my eating program even after the restriction period was over. To achieve that in everyday cooking, you need to stock your pantry and refrigerator with spices, herbs, and condiments. Here are my suggestions:

▷ PANTRY

Anchovy paste: We don't use this ingredient that often, but when a recipe calls for it, nothing else will really do. *Note: this is very high in sodium.*

Artificial sweetener: Don't cook with aspartame (Equal or NutraSweet) because it breaks down under high temperatures. It is perfectly fine for adding to hot beverages, sprinkling on fruit, or mixing into non-cooked recipes. For cooking, Splenda or Sweet 'N Low works better. Sweet 'N Low also makes a very good brown-sugar artificial sweetener.

Asian sauces and oils: At one time many of these sauces were considered exotic, but now just about every supermarket stocks them. They are highly distinctive in flavor, each adding an individual kick to the recipes in which they appear:

Asian chili paste with garlic	red chili paste
green curry sauce	red curry sauce
light soy sauce	sesame oil

Broth: Fat-free, low-sodium canned chicken and beef broth are absolute necessities for this cookbook. These broths provide both flavor and moisture without adding unnecessary fat or salt.

Capers: Capers have a bright, almost metallic taste that really perks up simple dishes. They are bottled in brine, so you may want to rinse them off to reduce the sodium.

Clam juice or broth: A perfect low-fat liquid base for seafood soups and sauces. There are a number of good bottled brands, such as Doxee or Look's Atlantic Brand.

Cocoa, unsweetened: The key ingredient in low-fat hot cocoa, chocolate sauces, and desserts.

Concentrated broth: This is perfect for adding more beef or chicken flavor to sauces, soups, or stews. It's also more convenient than opening a whole can of broth for a recipe that only requires a couple of spoonfuls. Bovril and Knorr make very good concentrated broth in both chicken and beef flavors. *Note: this is high in sodium, but some stores carry reduced-sodium alternatives.*

Cooking spray: There are a lot of different brands available and I've found that most of them offer an easy, fat-free way to fry or sauté foods without adding oil. I always keep three flavors on hand—butter, canola oil, and olive oil.

Dried mushrooms: If you want to add a really intense mushroom flavor to soups or stews, throw some of these in just as they are. For quicker-cooking dishes, I soak them in boiling water, then strain the water and use both the softened mushrooms and the liquid. You can find plain white dried mushrooms, as well as more exciting ones, such as dried shiitakes, dried morels, dried chanterelles, and dried mixed exotic mushrooms in most supermarkets.

Dried spices and herbs: Keeping a variety of these dried and/or ground flavorings on hand is a must for the recipes in this cookbook. You probably already have a lot of them, so it just means a bit of filling in.

allspice	celery seed	cumin
basil	chili powder	curry powder
cardamom	cinnamon	dill
cayenne pepper	cloves (whole and ground)	fennel seeds
celery flakes	coriander	garam masala
celery salt	cream of tartar	garlic powder

ginger	oregano	saffron threads
lemon-pepper	paprika (sweet and hot)	tarragon
mint	parsley	thyme
nutmeg	red pepper flakes	turmeric
onion flakes		

Evaporated skim or fat-free milk: This is a wonderful ingredient when you want a soup or a sauce to be slightly richer or thicker, but don't want to add carbs or calories. It reduces down very nicely and caramelizes beautifully.

Flavor extracts: These are lots fun to experiment with, and they don't add any extra calories. We found a number of sites on the Web that offer an incredible variety—for example, www.Penzey's.com and www.spicebarn.com. Of course, you'll want vanilla, but we also suggest coconut and almond.

Garlic: To me, you can never have too much garlic—but don't worry, I did use restraint when I developed these recipes. I always keep a bunch of fresh heads of garlic around and when I need some, I smack a few garlic cloves with the flat of a knife, then peel and chop them. If you prefer to use a garlic press or mince them in a mini-chopper, feel free. (*Here's Michele's hint: to take the garlic smell off your fingers, hold the blade of a metal knife in your fingers—both hands—and run it under cold water. It's magic!*)

Horseradish: Talk about pungent! This is one of the best perker-uppers we know. It goes especially well with creamy sauces. I use prepared, bottled white horseradish and drain it well before adding it to recipes.

Juices: While fresh citrus juices are preferable, sometimes you just don't have fresh fruit in the house or you don't want to cut up a whole lemon or lime just to squeeze out a spoonful. I always keep bottles of orange, lemon, and lime juices as well as small cans of tomato juice in my pantry.

Mayonnaise: Nothing takes the place of mayo in sauces and cold salads. That's why it's great that all of the manufacturers now offer light and fat-free versions. We tried a lot of different ones and do prefer the light (25 calories per tablespoon) over the fat-free (10 calories per tablespoon)—it's a matter of taste.

Mustard: While this condiment is quite pungent straight from the jar, it mellows out deliciously during the cooking process. We use both dijon and whole-grain mustard in our recipes.

Roasted red peppers: Sure, you can char and peel fresh peppers, but why bother? Many traditional Spanish-accented recipes call for bottled roasted red peppers.

Sauces: There are a number of condiment sauces that can really liven up a recipe. I always keep some brand of hot sauce as well as Worcestershire sauce on hand.

Shallots: Fresh shallots are probably the subtlest member of the onion family. I always keep a bag of them in stock. Shallots are so convenient to use—I admit, sometimes when a recipe calls for a small amount of onion, instead of peeling a whole big onion I use a couple of cloves of shallot instead.

Soy nuts: After you're through the soft-food stage and you want a bit of crunch, try toasted soy nuts. I grind them in my mini-processor and use them as a crunchy topping, or use them instead of breadcrumbs with egg substitute to make a low-carb coating for fish, pork, or chicken. They are very high in protein. You can find them in some supermarkets and all health food shops.

Tomatoes, canned: While some recipes call for fresh tomatoes, in many cases we've stipulated using different types of canned tomatoes. Here are some suggestions:

> diced tomatoes, 14.5-ounce can
> Italian-style plum tomatoes, 28-ounce can
> stewed tomatoes, 14.5-ounce can
> sun-dried tomato paste in a tube
> tomato paste in a tube
> tomato paste, 6-ounce can
> tomato sauce, 8- or 14.5-ounce can
> tomato puree, 14.5- or 28-ounce can
> whole peeled tomatoes, 28-ounce can

Unsweetened low-fat or light coconut milk: This is another one of those surprising ingredients that we found when we were looking for something that would add thickness and richness to a dish without adding a lot of fat or calories. Don't worry; the coconut flavor is very subtle.

Wasabi: Although once referred to as Japanese mustard, wasabi is really a type of ground horseradish. You can buy it in powder form and mix it with water, but I buy it as a paste in a handy tube.

Wines: I know that most food experts say that you shouldn't cook with any wine you wouldn't drink. Well, call me a philistine, but if I don't have an opened bottle of wine around, I use commercial brands of cooking wine. You'll need dry white wine, dry red wine, dry sherry, and dry vermouth.

Vinegars: I love having a variety of vinegars to play with. Our recipes call for balsamic, cider, and red wine vinegars, as well as Asian rice vinegar. But why stop there? Try raspberry vinegar or sherry pepper vinegar, too.

▷ REFRIGERATOR

Artificial butter spray: I always keep a bottle of I Can't Believe It's Not Butter spray in my fridge for spritzing on steamed vegetables or mixing into mashed cauliflower.

Cheddar cheese, low fat: This is just fine for cooking purposes, and some is even okay for eating plain. Cabot makes a 50 percent low-fat cheddar that is fine for cooking or eating, but I will only use their 75 percent low-fat cheddar for cooking.

Cream cheese, fat free: While you probably wouldn't want to eat this plain, as a cooking ingredient it adds a luscious, creamy richness to a number of our recipes.

Egg substitute: When a recipe calls for eggs, I generally use egg substitute (such as Egg Beaters or Better 'N Eggs). When I need whipped egg whites, I usually use egg substitute whites (like All Whites or other brands).

Fresh herbs: I love using fresh herbs, especially in quick-cooking recipes. Since most recipes just call for small amounts, I freeze my fresh herbs in zippered plastic snack-size bags (with all the air pushed out), and I just use them as needed. *Don't defrost frozen herbs before using—they turn black and slimy.* Here are the ones I like to have on hand:

| basil | cilantro | parsley | sage | thyme |
| chive | mint | rosemary | tarrago | |

Fresh mushrooms: My mother once told me that I buy mushrooms the way other people by bread and milk. I absolutely love them. Fresh, firm white mushrooms have always been a staple in my house. Meredith did ask me to warn you that some people have gas problems with mushrooms.

Hot peppers: Michele introduced me to cooking with hot peppers, but I admit: I'm still a little timid. Look for small, firm jalapeño or serrano peppers.

Mozzarella, part skim: This is great for cooking Italian-style dishes when you want that melted, stretchy cheese experience. I even use it in omelets.

Parmesan: As far as we can tell, there is no hard grating cheese that is available in a low-fat version. Oh well. We justify including this tasty grated cheese by not using too much in any recipe.

Ricotta, fat free: I don't particularly like this for eating plain, but it works very well as an ingredient in our recipes. It's soft, creamy, and blends deliciously with herbs.

Sour cream, fat free: This is a perfect substitute for full-fat sour cream when it's used as we do, as an ingredient in recipes. It adds a very creamy, rich taste and texture without adding fat.

Swiss-type cheese, low fat: There are a number of nutty-tasting cheeses with holes that we generically refer to as Swiss. If you have a good cheese store or a well-stocked supermarket, you can usually find low-fat or light dammer, Gruyère, or domestic Swiss.

Yogurt, plain, fat-free: An absolute essential in making these recipes. And for eating by itself, I actually prefer it to the whole-fat or flavored yogurts—I mix a couple of spoonfuls of one of our fruit sauces into it and it tastes incredible.

Breakfast and Brunch

$\mathcal{E}$VEN THOUGH YOU are eating less, it is still important to eat breakfast. In the first weeks after surgery, when you are on a soft diet, remember that protein should be a key component of your meal. That's why we've included recipes for savory scrambled eggs and omelets that taste just as delicious pureed (if necessary) as they do whole.

Virtually all of these dishes use egg substitute to reduce your calorie intake. If you're careful not to overcook them, I think you can barely tell the difference between these scrambled eggs or omelets and ones made with whole eggs.

All of these recipes already call for truly delectable combinations of ingredients, but we encourage you to go ahead and experiment. Instead of broccoli, use asparagus or spinach. Play with different spices and herbs.

Best of all, there's no need to wait for breakfast to enjoy these tasty meals. I make many of these dishes for lunch and even for light dinners on a regular basis. You'll also find a number of other dishes in other sections of this cookbook that work well for breakfast or brunch. Try the Zucchini Flan (page 66), the Crustless Spinach and Cheese Quiche (page 60), or any of the incredibly luscious fruit smoothies in the Sweet Indulgences section (pages 159–160).

You'll find that breakfast and brunch can be just as interesting and satisfying as every other meal—so enjoy.

Note: The nutritional analyses are based on average portion size (*Others'* portions).

Breakfast and brunch dishes to wake your taste buds

Broccoli and Cheese Omelet

This is a delicious twist on the basic cheese omelet. The broccoli and shallots add a subtle sweetness to the nutty taste of Swiss.

1 cup broccoli florets, chopped
¼ cup shallots, minced
1 tablespoon water
butter-flavored cooking spray
1 cup egg substitute
4 ounces low-fat Swiss, diced
salt and pepper to taste

1. Mix broccoli, shallots, and water in a small microwaveable bowl. Cover with plastic wrap and microwave on HIGH for 3½ minutes, until broccoli is soft.
2. In a medium saucepan, heat cooking spray until hot but not smoking. Pour in egg substitute and swirl to coat bottom of pan.
3. Place ¼ diced cheese on one half of omelet and cover cheese with 2 tablespoons of broccoli mixture. Fold unfilled half of omelet over filling, lower heat, cover pan, and cook for 1–2 minutes, until cheese melts.
4. Slide omelet onto plate and keep warm. Re-spray skillet and repeat for all omelets. Add salt and pepper to taste.

MAKES 4 OMELETS

▷ **COOKING TIP:** For individual omelets, beat ¼ cup egg substitute with 1 teaspoon water until frothy.

SERVING GUIDELINES

▶ **FOR LAP-BAND:**
Weeks 1–4: Puree ½–1 omelet until smooth.
Weeks 5+: Serve ½–1 omelet as is.

▶ **FOR BYPASS:**
Weeks 1–4: Puree ½–1 omelet until smooth.
Weeks 5+: Serve ½ omelet as is.

▶ **FOR BPD-DS:**
Weeks 1–3: Puree ½–1 omelet until smooth.
Weeks 4+: Serve 1 omelet as is.

▶ **FOR OTHERS:**
Serve 1 omelet as is.

Calories: 122.21, **Protein:** 15.36g, **Fat:** 4.07g. **Carbohydrates:** 4.64g, **Cholesterol:** 15mg, **Fiber:** 0.05g, **Sodium:** 168.99mg

Garden Omelet

THIS IS A DELICIOUS, FRESH-TASTING WAY TO SERVE EGGS. USING THE MICROWAVE MAKES IT QUICK AND EASY.

½ cup zucchini, diced
½ cup plum tomatoes, diced
¾ cup fresh mushrooms, sliced thin
½ cup bell pepper, diced
1 tablespoon water
1 cup egg substitute
4 teaspoons water
butter-flavored cooking spray
4 ounces low-fat Swiss, sliced
salt and pepper to taste

1. In a microwaveable bowl, combine zucchini, tomatoes, mushrooms, and bell pepper with 1 tablespoon water. Cover tightly with plastic wrap and microwave on HIGH for 3–4 minutes.
2. In a small bowl, beat egg substitute with 4 teaspoons of water.
3. In a medium nonstick skillet, heat cooking spray until hot but not smoking. Pour in egg substitute and swirl to coat bottom of skillet.
4. Cut each slice of cheese into 4 pieces and arrange 4 pieces of cheese on one half of omelet. Cover cheese with 2–3 tablespoon of vegetable mixture and fold unfilled half of omelet over filling. Lower heat, cover pan, and cook for 1–2 minutes, until cheese melts.
5. Slide omelet onto plate and keep warm. Re-spray skillet and repeat for all omelets. Add salt and pepper to taste.

MAKES 4 OMELETS

▷ **COOKING TIP:** For individual omelets, beat ¼ cup egg substitute with 1 teaspoon water and a dash of freshly ground pepper.

SERVING GUIDELINES

▶ **FOR LAP-BAND:**
Weeks 1–4: Puree ½–1 omelet until smooth.
Weeks 5+: Serve ½–1 omelet as is.

▶ **FOR BYPASS:**
Weeks 1–4: Puree ½–1 omelet until smooth.
Weeks 5+: Serve ½–1 omelet as is.

▶ **FOR BPD-DS:**
Weeks 1–3: Puree ½–1 omelet until smooth.
Weeks 4+: Serve 1 omelet as is.

▶ **FOR OTHERS:**
Serve 1 omelet as is.

Calories: 126.43, **Protein:** 15.97g, **Fat:** 4.19g, **Carbohydrates:** 5.50g, **Cholesterol:** 15mg, **Fiber:** 0.99g, **Sodium:** 173.91mg

Omelet Italiano

I LIKE TO DESCRIBE THIS OMELET AS A BRUNCH PIZZA WITHOUT THE CRUST. AND, JUST AS WITH PIZZA, YOU CAN EXPERIMENT AND CHANGE THE FILLINGS: TRY BELL PEPPERS INSTEAD OF MUSHROOMS OR CANADIAN BACON INSTEAD OF SAUSAGE. BUT REMEMBER, THAT WILL CHANGE THE NUTRITIONAL NUMBERS, TOO.

butter-flavored cooking spray
2 low-fat turkey sausages
  (sweet Italian-style)
1 cup fresh mushrooms, sliced
  thin
½ cup onion, chopped
1 cup ripe plum tomatoes,
  chopped
2 teaspoons dried basil
1 cup egg substitute
1 teaspoon water
4 ounces part-skim mozzarella
  cheese, grated
salt and pepper to taste

1. In a large nonstick skillet, heat cooking spray until hot but not smoking. While the skillet is heating, remove sausage meat from casings; then brown it, breaking up the lumps, for 2 minutes.
2. Add mushrooms and onion and brown them, stirring for 2 minutes.
3. Stir in tomatoes and basil, lower heat, and cook, covered, for 3 minutes until tomatoes are softened.
4. Remove sausage-tomato mixture from skillet and keep warm. Then wash skillet, dry, and re-spray.
5. In a small bowl, combine ¼ cup egg substitute with 1 teaspoon water and beat well.
6. Heat skillet until hot but not smoking. Pour in egg substitute and swirl pan until entire bottom is covered. Place ¼ cheese on one half of egg and top with 3 tablespoons of sausage mixture.
7. Fold other side of omelet over filling, reduce heat, and cook, covered, for 2 minutes until cheese melts.
8. Slide omelet onto plate and keep warm. Re-spray pan and repeat for all omelets. Add salt and pepper to taste.

MAKES 4 SERVINGS

SERVING GUIDELINES

▶ **FOR LAP-BAND:**
  Weeks 1–4: Puree ½–1 omelet until smooth.
  Weeks 5+: Serve ½–1 omelet as is.

▶ **FOR BYPASS:**
  Weeks 1–4: Puree ½–1 omelet until smooth
  Weeks 5+: Serve ½–1 omelet as is.

▶ **FOR BPD-DS:**
  Weeks 1–3: Puree ½–1 omelet until smooth.
  Weeks 4+: Serve 1 omelet as is.

▶ **FOR OTHERS:**
  Serve 1 omelet as is.

Calories: 193.38, **Protein:** 19.44g, **Fat:** 9.09g, **Carbohydrates:** 7.14g, **Cholesterol:** 42.50mg, **Fiber:** 1.27g, **Sodium:** 706.50mg

Omelet à la Quebec

I FIRST TASTED THIS OMELET ON A TRIP TO CANADA AND MADE IT PART OF MY COOKING REPERTOIRE AS SOON AS WE RETURNED. OF COURSE, MICHELE AND I ADAPTED IT FOR THIS BOOK, BUT IT TASTES JUST AS GOOD.

1½ cups fresh mushrooms, sliced thin
1 tablespoon water plus 1 teaspoon water
4 ounces (4 thin slices) cooked turkey breast, torn in small pieces
1 cup egg substitute
butter-flavored cooking spray
4 ounces low-fat cheddar cheese, diced
salt and pepper to taste

1. Place mushrooms and 1 tablespoon water in a small microwaveable bowl, cover with plastic wrap, and microwave on HIGH for 3 minutes. Mix turkey pieces into cooked mushrooms.
2. In a separate bowl, beat ¼ cup egg substitute with 1 teaspoon water.
3. In a medium nonstick skillet, heat cooking spray until hot but not smoking. Pour in egg substitute, swirling pan until entire bottom is covered.
4. Scatter ¼ cheese on one half of omelet and cover cheese with 2 tablespoons of mushroom-turkey mixture.
5. Fold unfilled half of omelet over filling; lower heat, cover, and cook for 1–2 minutes until cheese melts.
6. Slide omelet out of pan and keep warm. Add salt and pepper to taste. Re-spray skillet and repeat for all omelets

MAKES 4 SERVINGS

SERVING GUIDELINES

▶ **FOR LAP-BAND:**
Weeks 1–4: Puree ½–1 omelet until smooth.
Weeks 5+: Serve ½–1 omelet as is.

▶ **FOR BYPASS:**
Weeks 1–4: Puree ½–1 omelet until smooth.
Weeks 5+: Serve ½–1 omelet as is.

▶ **FOR BPD-DS:**
Weeks 1–3: Puree ½–1 omelet until smooth.
Weeks 4+: Serve 1 omelet as is.

▶ **FOR OTHERS:**
Serve 1 omelet as is.

Calories: 126.19, **Protein:** 23.26g, **Fat:** 2.11g, **Carbohydrates:** 3.19g, **Cholesterol:** 19.53mg, **Fiber:** 1.82g, **Sodium:** 347.80mg

Scrambled Eggs à la Quebec

THESE ARE THE SAME INGREDIENTS AS IN THE OMELET À LA QUEBEC (PAGE 29), JUST SCRAMBLED INSTEAD. YOU MIGHT WANT TO TRY THIS RECIPE FOR THE FIRST FEW WEEKS AFTER SURGERY, THEN SWITCH TO THE OMELET LATER ON.

1 cup egg substitute
1 teaspoon water
4 ounces low-fat cheddar
  cheese, diced
butter-flavored cooking spray
1½ cups fresh mushrooms,
  sliced thin
4 ounces (4 thin slices) cooked
  low-salt turkey, torn in small
  pieces
salt and pepper to taste

1. Beat egg substitute with 1 teaspoon water and stir in cheese.
2. In a medium nonstick skillet, heat cooking spray until hot but not smoking. Sauté mushrooms for about 1–2 minutes until lightly browned.
3. In a food processor, puree cooked mushrooms and turkey until smooth.
4. Re-spray skillet and, over moderate heat, add mushroom-turkey puree, then egg-cheese mixture, stirring constantly to form small curds for 1–2 minutes or desired degree of doneness. Add salt and pepper to taste.

MAKES 4 SERVINGS

SERVING GUIDELINES

▶ **FOR LAP-BAND:**
  Weeks 1+: Serve ¼–½ cup as is.

▶ **FOR BYPASS:**
  Weeks 1+: Serve ¼–½ cup as is.

▶ **FOR BPD-DS:**
  Weeks 1+: Serve ½ cup as is.

▶ **FOR OTHERS:**
  Serve ½ cup as is.

Calories: 126.19, **Protein:** 23.26g, **Fat:** 2.11g, **Carbohydrates:** 3.19g, **Cholesterol:** 19.53mg, **Fiber:** 1.82g, **Sodium:** 347.80mg

Scrambled Eggs with Ham and Cheese

YES, THERE IS A WAY TO EAT THE ALL-AMERICAN FAVORITE BREAKFAST COMBINATION AND STILL EAT THE WAY YOU SHOULD. HERE IT IS.

1 cup egg substitute
1 tablespoon water
4 ounces low-fat cheddar
* cheese, diced*
4 ounces low-fat sliced ham,
* finely minced*
butter-flavored cooking spray
salt and pepper to taste

1. In a small bowl, beat egg substitute with water until frothy. Stir in cheese and ham.
2. In a medium nonstick skillet, heat cooking spray until hot but not smoking. Pour in egg mixture, stirring constantly for 1–2 minutes until eggs form small curds that are soft but not runny and cheese melts. Add salt and pepper to taste.

MAKES 4 SERVINGS

SERVING GUIDELINES

▶ FOR LAP-BAND:
  Weeks 1+: Serve ¼–½ cup as is.

▶ FOR BYPASS:
  Weeks 1+: Serve ¼–½ cup as is.

▶ FOR BPD-DS:
  Weeks 1+: Serve ½ cup as is.

▶ FOR OTHERS:
  Serve ½ cup as is.

Calories: 108.25, **Protein:** 17.58g, **Fat:** 3.03g, **Carbohydrates:** 1.82g, **Cholesterol:** 19.56mg, **Fiber:** 0g, **Sodium:** 617.67mg

Vegetable Frittata

Whenever I'm having company for brunch, I make this dish. It's like a salad and an omelet all in one.

1 cup egg substitute
2 tablespoons water
cooking spray
1 cup zucchini, cut into ½-inch cubes
1 cup fresh mushrooms, cut into ½-inch cubes
½ cup onion, sliced thin
½ cup bell pepper, seeded and cut into ½-inch cubes
½ cup Parmesan cheese, grated
salt and pepper to taste

1. In medium bowl, beat egg substitute with water until well mixed.
2. In large nonstick skillet heat cooking spray until hot but not smoking. Sauté zucchini, mushrooms, onion, and pepper for 3–5 minutes until lightly browned and softened.
3. Pour egg substitute over vegetable mixture. Lower heat, cover skillet, and cook for 1–2 minutes until set.
4. Sprinkle cheese on top of frittata and place under preheated broiler for 1–2 minutes until cheese browns. Add salt and pepper to taste.

Makes 4 servings

SERVING GUIDELINES

▶ **FOR LAP-BAND:**
Weeks 1–4: Puree ¼–½ cup frittata until smooth.
Weeks 5+: Serve ¼–½ cup frittata as is.

▶ **FOR BYPASS:**
Weeks 1–4: Puree ¼–½ cup frittata until smooth.
Weeks 5+: Serve ¼–½ cup frittata as is.

▶ **FOR BPD-DS:**
Weeks 1–3: Puree ½ cup frittata until smooth.
Weeks 4+: Serve ½–¼ cup of frittata as is.

▶ **FOR OTHERS:**
Serve ¼. frittata as is.

Calories: 108.34, **Protein:** 12.46g, **Fat:** 3.92g, **Carbohydrates:** 6.01g, **Cholesterol:** 9.88mg, **Fiber:** 1.28g, **Sodium:** 335.35mg

Deviled Egg Salad

TANGY AND SLIGHTLY SPICY, THIS IS A NICE CHANGE FOR BREAKFAST OR LUNCH. YOU COULD EVEN PACK IT FOR LUNCH OR A SNACK AT WORK.

4 medium eggs
2 tablespoons low-fat mayonnaise
1 teaspoon dried minced onion
2 teaspoons Dijon mustard
2 teaspoons sweet or hot paprika
salt and pepper to taste
hot sauce to taste (optional)

1. Place eggs in a small pot, cover with water, and bring to a boil over high heat. Cook for 18 minutes.
2. Run cold water over eggs for 1–2 minutes until eggs are cool enough to handle.
3. Peel eggs and cut in quarters.
4. Place eggs and all other ingredients in food processor or mini-chopper and blend for 15 seconds until almost smooth. Add salt and pepper, and hot sauce to taste.

MAKES 4 SERVINGS

SERVING GUIDELINES

▶ **FOR LAP-BAND:**
 Weeks 1+: Serve ¼ cup as is.

▶ **FOR BYPASS:**
 Weeks 1+: Serve ¼ cup as is.

▶ **FOR BPD-DS:**
 Weeks 1+: Serve ¼ cup as is.

▶ **FOR OTHERS:**
 Serve ¼ cup as is.

Calories: 94.69, **Protein:** 6.60g, **Fat:** 5.84g, **Carbohydrates:** 3.81g, **Cholesterol:** 212.55mg, **Fiber:** 0.30g, **Sodium:** 147.64mg

Soup It Up

WHEN MEREDITH FIRST showed me the guideline menus suggested for the first weeks after surgery, I was pleased to see that they included soup. I love soup. But not the kind that comes in cans. I love homemade soups, and I bet you will, too.

Some of our soup recipes are designed to be eaten as purees; all others taste great pureed but are equally good when you serve them just the way you cook them—thick with the textures of different chopped ingredients.

In this section, we offer you a fantastic selection of soups—smooth, cold summer soups; satisfying meal-in-a-bowl soups; even rich chowders and creamed soups. There are vegetable-based soups, chicken-and-turkey-based soups, plus a lot of wonderful seafood soups. And they are all high in protein, low in calories, and low in carbohydrates.

It took a lot of testing and ingenuity, but we came up with a variety of ways to add creaminess or richness to many of our soup recipes. Using unsweetened light coconut milk or evaporated skim milk, we added thickness without adding distinctive flavor. Plain, fat-free yogurt or sour cream allowed us to add tangy creaminess to other recipes. And how did we make a full-bodied chowder without potatoes? We discovered that if we cook cauliflower very soft, then cube some of it and mash some more, then add it in, we got just the result we were looking for.

Everlovin'
spoonfuls
for every
season

So why relegate soup to just the beginning of a meal? Some of our soups are meals in themselves—they make great light dinners. Or, if you have access to a microwave at work, why not make your favorite recipe ahead of time and brown-bag some home-made soup for lunch? Even if you don't have a microwave, bring in one of our cold soups. Soups also make terrifically satisfying snacks—you know, those healthy snacks that we're allowed to have once a day.

And, yes, we even offer a version of Mom's chicken soup—it's called Mother-in-Law Soup—I guess 'cause she uses a lot of garlic to keep her precious son from wanting to get too amorous.

Note: The nutritional analyses are based on an average portion size (*Others'* portions).

Bengali Chicken and Vegetable Soup

CHICKEN SOUP WITH AN EXOTIC ACCENT: THICKENED WITH VEGETABLES, ENRICHED WITH COCONUT MILK, AND SPARKED WITH CINNAMON, GINGER, AND JALAPEÑO.

1 14-ounce can of unsweet-
  ened light coconut milk
1 medium onion, chopped
1 garlic clove, minced
¼ teaspoon dried thyme
¼ cup fresh parsley
2 whole cloves
½ teaspoon cinnamon
1 tablespoon fresh ginger,
  finely minced
1 small fresh jalapeño pepper,
  seeded and finely chopped
1 14.5-ounce can of fat-free,
  low-sodium chicken broth
½ pound skinless chicken
  breast, diced
½ pound cauliflower florets
½ pound broccoli florets
1 large carrot, sliced
salt and pepper to taste

1. In a large soup pot, combine coconut milk, onion, garlic, thyme, parsley, cloves, cinnamon, ginger, and jalapeño. Bring to a simmer, uncovered, stirring occasionally, for 15–20 minutes until thickened. Remove whole cloves.
2. Stir in chicken broth, chicken, cauliflower, broccoli, and carrot. Cover pot, and simmer for 1 hour. Add salt and pepper to taste.

MAKES 4 SERVINGS

SERVING GUIDELINES

▶ **FOR LAP-BAND:**
  Weeks 1–4: Puree ½ cup.
  Weeks 5+: Serve ½–1 cup as is.

▶ **FOR BYPASS:**
  Weeks 1–4: Puree ½ cup.
  Weeks 5+: Serve ½–1 cup as is.

▶ **FOR BPD-DS:**
  Weeks 1+: Serve ½–1 cup as is.

▶ **FOR OTHERS:**
  Serve 1 cup as is.

Calories: 218.99, **Protein:** 17.19g, **Fat:** 7.86g, **Carbohydrates:** 14.65g, **Cholesterol:** 32.89mg, **Fiber:** 4.36g, **Sodium:** 521.22mg

Chicken and Mushroom Soup

To me, this is the ultimate "Mommy-loves-me" food. Rich and creamy with the earthy, autumn taste of fresh and dried mushrooms, this is pure comfort in a bowl.

cooking spray

1½ cups onion, chopped

3 garlic cloves, minced

1 pound fresh white mush-
   rooms, chopped

½ teaspoon dried tarragon

1 bay leaf

¼ teaspoon dried thyme

½ cup white wine

½ pound boneless, skinless
   chicken breast, quartered

2 14.5-ounce cans of fat-free,
   low-sodium chicken broth

⅓ cup dried shiitake mushrooms (about ½ ounce)

¼ cup fat-free sour cream

2 tablespoons fresh chives,
   chopped, or 1 tablespoon
   dried chives

salt and pepper to taste

1. Coat the bottom of a large soup pot with cooking spray and sauté onion, garlic, and fresh mushrooms over medium heat. Cover and cook for 10 minutes, stirring occasionally.
2. Add tarragon, bay leaf, thyme, and wine, stirring and scraping bottom of pot to loosen brown bits.
3. Lower heat and add chicken, chicken broth, and dried mushrooms. Cover and simmer for 30 minutes.
4. Discard bay leaf and stir in sour cream.
5. Puree soup in batches in food processor until smooth. Add salt and pepper to taste, and top with chives.

Makes 4 servings

SERVING GUIDELINES

▶ **FOR LAP-BAND:**
   Weeks 1+: Serve ½–1 cup as is.

▶ **FOR BYPASS:**
   Weeks 1+: Serve ½–1 cup as is.

▶ **FOR BPD-DS:**
   Weeks 1+: Serve ½–1 cup as is.

▶ **FOR OTHERS:**
   Serve 1 cup as is.

Calories: 238.77, **Protein:** 21.46g, **Fat:** 1.49g, **Carbohydrates:** 32.48g, **Cholesterol:** 35.39mg, **Fiber:** 5.84g, **Sodium:** 682.87mg

Chicken Artichoke Soup

THIS RECIPE IS A GREAT WAY TO USE UP YOUR LEFTOVER CHICKEN. IT'S INCREDIBLY EASY TO MAKE BUT TASTES LIKE FINE FRENCH COOKING—SMOOTH, RICH, AND SOPHISTICATED. SERVE IT HOT OR COLD.

1 14-ounce can of artichoke hearts in brine, drained well

2 ounces soft or silken tofu

3 tablespoons grated Parmesan cheese

1½ tablespoons fresh lemon juice

¾ teaspoon dried tarragon

2 teaspoons grated lemon peel

2 garlic cloves, minced

¼ teaspoon ground nutmeg

¼ teaspoon chili powder

2 cups fat-free, low-sodium chicken broth

½ pound cooked skinless, boneless chicken breast, cubed

1. Puree artichoke hearts in food processor until chunky.
2. Add remaining ingredients and puree until smooth.
3. Pour into large pot, cover, and simmer over low flame for 10 minutes.

MAKES 4 SERVINGS

SERVING GUIDELINES

▶ **FOR LAP-BAND:**
Weeks 1+: Serve ½–1 cup as is.

▶ **FOR BYPASS:**
Weeks 1+: Serve ½–1 cup as is.

▶ **FOR BPD-DS:**
Weeks 1+: Serve ½–1 cup as is.

▶ **FOR OTHERS:**
Serve 1 cup as is.

Calories: 161.67, **Protein:** 21.85g, **Fat:** 3.35g, **Carbohydrates:** 11.53g, **Cholesterol:** 46.62mg, **Fiber:** 1.68g, **Sodium:** 741.05mg

Mother-in-Law Soup

YOU'VE HEARD OF MAMA'S CHICKEN SOUP? WELL, THIS IS THE SPANISH MOTHER-IN-LAW'S VERSION, GOLDEN WITH SAFFRON AND GUTSY WITH GARLIC. I SUBSTITUTED PROSCIUTTO FOR THE TRADITIONAL SERRANO HAM, BECAUSE IT'S EASIER TO FIND IN THE MARKET.

olive oil cooking spray
4 large garlic cloves, minced
1 ounce prosciutto, diced
1 teaspoon sweet paprika
¼ teaspoon ground cumin
¼ teaspoon freshly ground
  pepper
⅛ teaspoon saffron threads
2 14.5-ounce cans fat-free,
  low-sodium chicken broth
4 large eggs
salt to taste

1. In a large nonstick saucepan, heat cooking spray until hot but not smoking. Sauté garlic for 1 minute. Add prosciutto and paprika, and sauté for 30 more seconds.
2. Stir in cumin, pepper, and saffron, add broth, and bring to a boil.
3. Cover pan, reduce heat, and simmer for 20 minutes.
4. One at a time, carefully break eggs into soup and simmer for 3 minutes until whites are set. Add salt to taste.

MAKES 4 SERVINGS

SERVING GUIDELINES

▶ **FOR LAP-BAND:**
  Weeks 1–4: Puree ¼–½ cup
    soup with 1 poached egg.
  Weeks 5+: Serve ¼–½ cup soup
    topped with 1 poached egg.

▶ **FOR BYPASS:**
  Weeks 1–4: Puree ¼–½ cup
    soup with 1 poached egg.
  Weeks 5+: Serve ¼–½ cup soup
    topped with 1 poached egg.

▶ **FOR BPD-DS:**
  Weeks 1–3: Puree ½ cup soup
    with 1 poached egg.
  Weeks 4+: Serve ½–1 cup soup
    topped with 1 poached egg.

▶ **FOR OTHERS:**
  Serve 1 cup soup topped with 1
    poached egg.

Calories: 106.94, **Protein:** 9.56g, **Fat:** 5.89g, **Carbohydrates:** 4.08g, **Cholesterol:** 216.25mg, **Fiber:** 0.24g, **Sodium:** 876.60mg

Cold Shrimp Soup

THIS IS ANOTHER ONE OF THOSE QUICK AND EASY SOUPS THAT TASTES LIKE YOU SPENT HOURS COOKING IT. AND, BECAUSE IT'S PUREED, YOU CAN BUY THE SMALLEST, LEAST EXPENSIVE SHRIMP AND NO ONE CAN TELL THE DIFFERENCE.

2 cups low-fat buttermilk
1½ teaspoons dry mustard
¼ packet artificial sweetener
½ pound cooked shrimp, peeled and cleaned
½ cup cucumber, peeled, seeded, and chopped
1 tablespoon fresh chives, minced
salt and pepper to taste

1. In a food processor, combine all ingredients and puree until smooth.
2. Chill for 1 hour in refrigerator before serving. Add salt and pepper to taste.

MAKES 4 SERVINGS

SERVING GUIDELINES

▶ **FOR LAP-BAND:**
Weeks 1+: Serve ½–1 cup soup as is.

▶ **FOR BYPASS:**
Weeks 1+: Serve ½–1 cup soup as is.

▶ **FOR BPD-DS:**
Weeks 1+: Serve ½–1 cup soup as is.

▶ **FOR OTHERS:**
Serve 1 cup soup as is.

Calories: 90.34, **Protein:** 11.50g, **Fat:** 1.93g, **Carbohydrates:** 6.76g, **Cholesterol:** 68.23mg, **Fiber:** 0.25g, **Sodium:** 410.33mg

Creamy Shrimp Chowder

As you read down the list of ingredients for this recipe, you may be surprised by the cauliflower. Trust me, it works! It thickens like potato (which is in most chowders) without adding a lot of carbs. Note: Pureed, this soup tastes like the most outrageous shrimp bisque.

1 cup cauliflower, coarsely cut up
cooking spray
¼ cup medium onion, chopped
1 teaspoon garlic, chopped
1 ounce low-fat ham, finely diced
¼ teaspoon lemon-pepper
1 8-ounce bottle clam juice
1 cup evaporated fat-free milk
½ pound large shrimp, shelled and de-veined, quartered
salt and pepper to taste

1. Pour 2 cups water into a large saucepan. Place cauliflower into steamer insert, put into saucepan, cover, and steam over medium heat for 20 minutes, or until very soft.
2. Coat the bottom of a large saucepan with cooking spray and cook onions and garlic over medium heat until soft, about 2 minutes.
3. Stir in ham and lemon-pepper, then add clam juice and evaporated milk.
4. Cook, stirring constantly, over medium flame until just barely boiling. Reduce heat to low and simmer, stirring occasionally, for 10 minutes (it should be slightly thickened).
5. Puree ½ cauliflower and add to soup, stir well, and simmer for 5 minutes.
6. Coarsely chop remaining cauliflower and add to soup.
7. Stir in shrimp and cook for 30 seconds to 1 minute until all shrimp pieces turn pink.

Makes 4 servings

SERVING GUIDELINES

▶ **FOR LAP-BAND:**
Weeks 1–4: Puree ½ cup.
Weeks 5–8: Put ½ cup soup in mini–chopper and process till shrimp is chopped.
Weeks 9+: Serve ½–1 cup as is.

▶ **FOR BYPASS:**
Weeks 1–4: Puree ½ cup.
Weeks 5–8: Put ½ cup soup in mini–chopper and process till shrimp is chopped.
Weeks 9+: Serve ½–1 cup as is.

▶ **FOR BPD-DS:**
Weeks 1–3: Puree ½ cup.
Weeks 4+: Serve ½–1 cup as is.

▶ **FOR OTHERS:**
Serve 1 cup as is.

Calories: 130.33, **Protein:** 21.96g, **Fat:** 1.53g, **Carbohydrates:** 10.56g, **Cholesterol:** 92.14mg, **Fiber:** 0.98g, **Sodium:** 646.69mg

Mock Manhattan Clam Chowder

I KNOW THAT CHOWDER TRADITIONALLY CONTAINS CHUNKS OF POTATOES, BUT I THINK ONCE YOU TASTE THIS CHOWDER, YOU WON'T MISS THEM. I USE EITHER CHOPPED FRESH CLAMS FROM MY LOCAL FISH MARKET OR FROZEN CHOPPED CLAMS—NEVER CANNED.

cooking spray
1 cup onion, cut in chunks
3 large cloves of garlic, minced
1 28-ounce can stewed tomatoes
½ pound cooked chopped fresh clams
2 tablespoons fresh basil or 2 teaspoons dried basil
⅛ teaspoon hot sauce (optional)
salt and pepper to taste

1. Coat bottom of large nonstick saucepan with cooking spray and cook onions and garlic over low heat, covered, for 5 minutes until just translucent.
2. Add all other ingredients, cover the pan, and simmer for 5 minutes or until heated through. Add salt and pepper to taste.

▷ **COOKING TIP:** Instead of simmering on the stovetop, you can heat in the microwave—pour into glass bowl covered with plastic wrap and microwave on HIGH for 4 minutes.

MAKES 4 SERVINGS

SERVING GUIDELINES

▶ **FOR LAP-BAND:**
Weeks 1–4: Puree ½ cup.
Weeks 5+: Serve ½–1 cup as is.

▶ **FOR BYPASS:**
Weeks 1–4: Not recommended.
Weeks 5+: Serve ½–1 cup as is.

▶ **FOR BPD-DS:**
Weeks 1–3: Puree ½ cup.
Weeks 4+: Serve ½–1 cup as is.

▶ **FOR OTHERS:**
Serve 1 cup as is.

Calories: 117.34, **Protein:** 9.49g, **Fat:** 0.63g, **Carbohydrates:** 17g, **Cholesterol:** 19.28mg, **Fiber:** 4.05g, **Sodium:** 60.40mg

Mussel Bisque

This is one of those elegant creamy soups that taste extravagantly rich, but it's not. Once you can start eating solid food, try making it without pureeing.

cooking spray
3 cloves garlic, minced
2 large shallots, minced
1 tablespoon fresh tarragon or
  ½ tablespoon dried
¾ cup dry white wine
2 pounds (about 40) mussels,
  scrubbed and de-bearded
1 8-ounce bottle clam juice
¾ cup fat-free sour cream
salt and pepper to taste

1. In a large stockpot, heat cooking spray over medium flame. Add garlic and shallots and cook for 2 minutes, stirring until soft and translucent.
2. Add tarragon and cook for 30 seconds more. Remove shallot-garlic mixture from pot and put it aside.
3. Add wine to pot, bring to a boil, add mussels, and steam, covered, for 5 minutes until mussels open.
4. With a slotted spoon, remove mussels and let cool slightly.
5. Add clam juice and reserved shallot-garlic mixture back into liquid in pot and simmer, covered, for 10 minutes.
6. Remove cooled mussels from shell and place all mussel meat, soup, and sour cream into a food processor. Puree until smooth. Add salt and pepper to taste.

Makes 4 servings

▷ **HINT:** You can serve this dish hot or cold.

SERVING GUIDELINES

▶ **FOR LAP-BAND:**
  Weeks 1–4: Serve ½ cup as is.
  Weeks 5+: Serve ½–1 cup as is.

▶ **FOR BYPASS:**
  Week 1–4: Serve ½ cup as is.
  Weeks 5+: Serve ½–1 cup as is.

▶ **FOR BPD-DS:**
  Week 1+: Serve ½–1 cup as is.

▶ **FOR OTHERS:**
  Serve 1 cup as is.

Calories: 234.31, **Protein:** 23.14g, **Fat:** 3.60g, **Carbohydrates:** 17.83g, **Cholesterol:** 52.30mg, **Fiber:** 0.05g, **Sodium:** 572.23mg

Mussels Madrilenos

THE SPANISH HAVE A FLAIR FOR COOKING WITH SHELLFISH. THIS RECIPE HAS ALL THE FLAVOR OF PAELLA, WITHOUT ALL THE CARBS FROM RICE.

olive oil cooking spray

2 large cloves garlic, chopped

½ cup of artichoke hearts in brine, drained and chopped

½ cup leeks, chopped (white and pale green stem)

½ cup ripe tomato, diced

2 teaspoons paprika

2 pinches saffron threads

¼ cup roasted red peppers, cut in strips

¼ cup white wine

1 cup clam juice

3 pounds (about 60) mussels, cleaned and de-bearded

salt and pepper to taste

1. In a large nonstick skillet, heat the cooking spray until hot but not smoking. Sauté garlic for 2 minutes until golden. Add artichokes and leeks and cook for 1 minute.
2. Add tomato, paprika, saffron, and roasted pepper strips, and cook over moderate heat, stirring for 5 minutes.
3. Stir wine and clam juice into tomato mixture, bring to a boil, and cook for 5 minutes.
4. Add mussels, cover skillet, and cook for 5–7 minutes until mussels open. Add salt and pepper to taste.

MAKES 4 SERVINGS

SERVING GUIDELINES

▶ **FOR LAP-BAND:**
  Weeks 1–4: Puree 6 cooked mussels with ¼ cup vegetables and broth.
  Weeks 5–8: Chop 6 cooked mussels, and serve with ¼ cup vegetables and broth.
  Weeks 9+: Serve 6–12 cooked mussels with ¼–½ cup vegetables and broth.

▶ **FOR BYPASS:**
  Weeks 1–4: Puree 6 cooked mussels with ¼ cup vegetables and broth.
  Weeks 5–8: Chop 6 cooked mussels, serve with ¼ cup vegetables and broth.
  Weeks 9+: Serve 6–12 cooked mussels with ¼–½ cup vegetables and broth.

▶ **FOR BPD-DS:**
  Weeks 1–3: Puree 6 cooked mussels with ¼ cup vegetables and broth
  Weeks 4+: Serve 6–12 cooked mussels with ½–1 cup vegetables and broth.

▶ **FOR OTHERS:**
  Serve 15 cooked mussels with 1 cup vegetables and broth.

Calories: 251.34, **Protein:** 30.03g, **Fat:** 5.63g, **Carbohydrates:** 13.62g, **Cholesterol:** 67.20mg, **Fiber:** 0.73g, **Sodium:** 794.34mg

Mussels Posillipo

SOMETIMES CALLED "ZUPPA DI MUSSELS," THIS TRADITIONAL SOUTHERN ITALIAN SOUP/MAIN DISH IS A DELICIOUSLY GARLICKY WAY TO PREPARE THIS VERSATILE SHELLFISH.

olive oil cooking spray
6 large garlic cloves, minced
2 tablespoons tomato paste
1 28-ounce can tomato puree
½ cup fresh basil, chopped
2 teaspoons dried oregano
½ cup clam juice
½ cup dry red wine
3 pounds mussels (about 60 mussels), cleaned and de-bearded
salt and pepper to taste

1. In a large nonstick skillet, heat cooking spray until hot but not smoking. Sauté garlic until soft, add tomato paste, and cook, stirring, until tomato paste browns.
2. Stir in tomato puree, basil, and oregano, lower heat, and cook, covered, about 5 minutes.
3. Add clam juice and wine and bring to a boil. Cook uncovered for 5 minutes.
4. Add mussels and cover skillet. Cook for 5–7 minutes until mussels open. Add salt and pepper to taste.

MAKES 4 SERVINGS

SERVING GUIDELINES

▶ **FOR LAP-BAND:**
Weeks 1–4: Puree 6 cooked mussels with ¼ cup soup.
Weeks 5–8: Chop 6 cooked mussels, and serve in ¼ cup soup.
Weeks 9+: Serve 6–12 cooked mussels in ¼–½ cup soup.

▶ **FOR BYPASS:**
Weeks 1–4: Puree 6 cooked mussels with ¼ cup soup.
Weeks 5–8: Chop 6 cooked mussels and serve in ¼ cup soup.
Weeks 9+: Serve 6–12 cooked mussels in ¼–½ cup soup.

▶ **FOR BPD-DS:**
Weeks 1–3: Puree 6 cooked mussels with ¼ cup soup.
Weeks 4+: Serve 6–12 cooked mussels in ½–1 cup soup.

▶ **FOR OTHERS:**
Serve 15 cooked mussels in 1 cup soup.

Calories: 326.99, **Protein:** 33.27g, **Fat:** 5.83g, **Carbohydrates:** 32.04g, **Cholesterol:** 67.20mg, **Fiber:** 4.62g, **Sodium:** 798.49mg

Mussels Steamed in Herbs and Wine

MICHELE AND I WENT TO A NEW MEDITERRANEAN RESTAURANT, WHERE I ORDERED A FANTASTIC MUSSEL DISH. NEEDLESS TO SAY, THE NEXT DAY WE TRIED TO RE-CREATE IT, KEEPING THE FAT AND CARBS LOW. IT MAKES A GREAT SOUP.

olive oil cooking spray
6 cloves garlic, minced
½ cup shallots, minced
2 tablespoons fresh tarragon
1 cup dry white wine
2 8-ounce bottles clam juice
3 pounds (about 60) mussels,
 cleaned and de-bearded
salt and pepper to taste

1. In a 4 to 5-quart pot, heat cooking spray over medium flame. Add garlic and shallots and cook, stirring, for 2 minutes until soft and translucent.
2. Stir in tarragon, and add wine and clam juice. Cover pot and bring to a boil.
3. Add mussels and steam, covered, for 5 minutes or until mussels open. Add salt and pepper to taste.

MAKES 4 SERVINGS

SERVING GUIDELINES

▶ **FOR LAP-BAND:**
Weeks 1–4: Puree 6 cooked mussels with ½ cup broth.
Weeks 5–8: Chop 6 cooked mussels and serve with ½ cup broth.
Weeks 9+: Serve 6–12 mussels with ½–1 cup broth.

▶ **FOR BYPASS:**
Weeks 1–4: Puree 6 cooked mussels with ½ cup broth.
Weeks 5–8: Chop 6 cooked mussels and serve with ½ cup broth.
Weeks 9+: Serve 6–12 mussels with ½–1 cup broth.

▶ **FOR BPD-DS:**
Weeks 1–3: Puree 6 cooked mussels with ½ cup broth.
Weeks 4+: Serve 6–12 cooked mussels with ½–1 cup broth.

▶ **FOR OTHERS:**
Serve 15 cooked mussels with 1 cup broth.

Calories: 320.16, **Protein:** 31.29g, **Fat:** 5.63g, **Carbohydrates:** 15.85g, **Cholesterol:** 67.20mg, **Fiber:** 0.26g, **Sodium:** 843.62mg

Southwestern Tomato Soup

HERE'S A HEARTY SOUP WITH A REAL TEX-MEX KICK. IF YOU LIKE IT EVEN SPICIER, DON'T BE AFRAID TO ADD MORE CHILI POWDER.

cooking spray
½ cup finely chopped onion
2 tablespoons garlic, minced
½ teaspoon chili powder
½ teaspoon ground cumin
½ teaspoon dried oregano
1 bay leaf
1 14.5-ounce can diced tomatoes with liquid
1 14.5-ounce can fat-free, low-sodium chicken broth
½ pound boneless, skinless turkey thighs (or any dark-meat turkey), cut up
salt and pepper to taste

1. Coat bottom of a large soup pot with cooking spray. Over medium heat, sauté onion and garlic for 3 minutes.
2. Stir in chili powder, cumin, oregano, and bay leaf. Add tomatoes, chicken broth, and turkey, and bring to a boil.
3. Lower heat, cover, and simmer for 45 minutes. Remove bay leaf.
4. Purée in batches. Add salt and pepper to taste.

MAKES 4 SERVINGS

SERVING GUIDELINES

▶ FOR LAP-BAND:
Weeks 1+: Serve ½–1 cup as is.

▶ FOR BYPASS:
Weeks 1+: Serve ½–1 cup as is.

▶ FOR BPD-DS:
Weeks 1+: Serve ½–1 cup as is.

▶ FOR OTHERS:
Serve 1 cup as is.

Calories: 122.99, **Protein:** 14.02g, **Fat:** 2.65g, **Carbohydrates:** 8.79g, **Cholesterol:** 39.12mg, **Fiber:** 2.35g, **Sodium:** 358.56mg

Tomato Yogurt Soup

THIS IS THE GROWN-UP VERSION OF THAT CREAMY TOMATO SOUP WE ALL LOVED AS KIDS. IT'S A LITTLE TANGIER, AND A BIT SPICIER, BUT JUST AS SATISFYING.

2 8-ounce containers plain,
  fat-free yogurt
1- to 2-pound can Italian plum
  tomatoes, drained
¼ teaspoon celery salt
¼ teaspoon curry powder
1 clove garlic, finely minced
salt and pepper to taste

1. Put all ingredients in a blender and puree until smooth. Add salt and pepper to taste.

MAKES 4 SERVINGS

▷ **HINT:** This soup can be served hot or cold (if serving hot, heat over low flame; do not boil).

SERVING GUIDELINES

▶ **FOR LAP-BAND:**
   Weeks 1+: Serve ½–1 cup soup
   as is.

▶ **FOR BYPASS:**
   Weeks 1+: Serve ½–1 cup soup
   as is.

▶ **FOR BPD-DS:**
   Weeks 1+: Serve ½–1 cup soup
   as is.

▶ **FOR OTHERS:**
   Serve 1 cup soup as is.

Calories: 104.57, **Protein:** 7.96g, **Fat:** 0.05g, **Carbohydrates:** 17.37g, **Cholesterol:** 2.50mg, **Fiber:** 1.95g, **Sodium:** 507.81mg

Chilled Tomato Soup with Basil

THIS IS A DELECTABLE, REFRESHING SOUP THAT HAS A SOPHISTICATED SUMMER APPEAL.
YOU CAN ALSO SERVE IT HOT.

*1 28-ounce can of whole,
peeled tomatoes
1 cup plain, fat-free yogurt
1 teaspoon ground cumin
2 teaspoons Worcestershire
sauce
1½ cups fresh basil leaves*

1. Puree tomatoes in food processor until smooth.
2. Using a fine-mesh strainer, strain tomato puree over bowl, pressing solids to get as much liquid as possible. Then discard seeds and solids left in strainer.
3. Pour strained tomato puree back in food processor, add yogurt, cumin, Worcestershire sauce, and 1 cup of basil leaves, and puree until smooth.
4. For garnish, finely mince remaining ½ cup of basil and sprinkle on top of individual servings.

MAKES 4 SERVINGS

SERVING GUIDELINES

▶ **FOR LAP-BAND:**
Weeks 1+: Serve ½–1 cup as is.

▶ **FOR BYPASS:**
Weeks 1+: Serve ½–1 cup as is.

▶ **FOR BPD-DS:**
Weeks 1+: Serve ½–1 cup as is.

▶ **FOR OTHERS:**
Serve 1 cup as is.

Calories: 93.47, **Protein:** 7.40g, **Fat:** 1.12g, **Carbohydrates:** 15.70g, **Cholesterol:** 1.25mg, **Fiber:** 5.16g, **Sodium:** 440.42mg

Vegetables—Not Just an Aside

*W*E'VE ALL HEARD the admonition to "eat your vegetables." But after weight reduction surgery, this can be a problem, as some people have trouble digesting certain vegetables in the weeks after surgery. So, in most of the recipe guidelines for this section, you'll notice that these dishes are not recommended for the first three to four weeks.

Of course, food tolerances can be very different for each person—for example, if you're like me, you'll be able to eat anything without any digestive sensitivity. If you're worried about adding vegetables back into your diet, try steaming and pureeing a small amount of various plain vegetables and see how you react. If it causes bloating or gas, don't try it again for at least two weeks to a month.

Okay, all caveats aside, let me tell you about these incredible vegetable recipes. They really put to rest the idea that vegetables are boring. We've used a variety of vegetables—mostly fresh, but we use a couple of frozen veggies in one or two recipes. You'll be amazed at the many different ways we've created to cook them—from simple purees to rich gratins, gutsy casseroles to delicate little pancakes, and even a spicy curry.

And here's where our ingenuity really paid off. We know that many people love mashed potatoes. But soft, buttery mashed potatoes are a real no-no when it comes to carbs and calories. After mashing many different veggies, we finally discovered celery root,

Vegetables
that work
with a meal
or as a meal

also known as celeriac. When you cook it with skim milk, then puree it in your food processor with a little bit of Benecol or other light heart-healthy margarine, it is sure to please any potato lover.

A lot of our veggie recipes (I think there are two exceptions) include protein from low-fat or fat-free cheeses, egg or egg white substitute, and soy nuts, which means they can be much more than just side dishes. You can eat them as delicious vegetarian main dishes for lunch or dinner. Some are even terrific for breakfast or brunch—such as Crustless Spinach and Cheese Quiche (page 60) or Zucchini Flan (page 66). Just be sure to check the protein levels to make sure that you're getting the amount you need every day.

So, go ahead and "eat your vegetables" as soon as you can. They really make any eating program more varied, not to mention better balanced.

Note: The nutritional analyses are based on an average portion size (*Others'* portions).

Broccoli and Cheddar Gratin

I LOVE PAIRING VEGETABLES WITH CHEESE, AND THE ADDITION OF SOY NUTS GIVES THIS DISH A BIT OF UNEXPECTED CRUNCH (NOT TO MENTION AN EXTRA MEASURE OF PROTEIN).

4 cups broccoli florets
butter-flavored cooking spray
2 large garlic cloves, minced
¼ teaspoon crushed red pepper
  flakes
¼ cup low-fat, low-sodium veg-
  etable broth
½ pound low-fat cheddar
  cheese, grated
¼ cup ground soy nuts

1. Preheat oven to 400°F.
2. In a pot fitted with a steamer basket, steam broccoli over ¾ cup water, covered, for 15 minutes until soft.
3. Coat a large skillet with cooking spray and sauté garlic and red pepper flakes over medium heat for 1 minute until just fragrant. Remove from heat and stir in broccoli, broth, and ¼ cup grated cheese.
4. Coat a 2-quart casserole with cooking spray and pour in broccoli-cheese mixture. Top with remaining cheese and sprinkle with ground soy nuts. Then spray top with cooking spray.
5. Bake for about 12 minutes until cheese is melted and topping is golden.

MAKES 4 SERVINGS

SERVING GUIDELINES

► **FOR LAP-BAND:**
  Weeks 1–4: Not recommended.
  Weeks 5+: Serve ¼–½ cup broccoli mixture as is.

► **FOR BYPASS:**
  Weeks 1–4: Not recommended.
  Weeks 5+: Serve ¼–½ cup broccoli mixture as is.

► **FOR BPD-DS:**
  Weeks 1–4: Not recommended.
  Weeks 5+: Serve ¼–½ cup broccoli mixture as is.

► **FOR OTHERS:**
  Serve 1 cup broccoli mixture as is.

Calories: 172.28, **Protein:** 19.92g, **Fat:** 7.05g, **Carbohydrates:** 9.15g, **Cholesterol:** 11.88mg, **Fiber:** 1.96g, **Sodium:** 428.78mg

Broccoli Soufflé

A SOUFFLÉ IS AN ELEGANT DISH, BUT REMEMBER, ONCE YOU TAKE IT OUT OF THE OVEN, SERVE IT IMMEDIATELY OR ELSE IT WILL COLLAPSE.

1 10-ounce package frozen
   chopped broccoli, thawed
   and drained
butter-flavored cooking spray
1 cup onion, finely chopped
2 garlic cloves, minced
½ teaspoon hot sauce
1 cup skim evaporated milk
½ cup egg substitute
¼ cup Parmesan cheese,
   grated
6 tablespoons egg white
   substitute
¼ teaspoon cream of tartar
salt and pepper to taste

1. Preheat oven to 400°F.
2. Place broccoli in a double layer of paper towels and squeeze dry.
3. In a medium skillet, heat cooking spray, add onions and garlic, and cook until onion is soft, about 5 minutes. Lower heat and add hot sauce and milk. Simmer for 4 minutes, stirring occasionally.
4. Place egg substitute in a small bowl and gradually add ½ cup of the hot milk-onion mixture, stirring constantly with a whisk.
5. Add egg mixture back into skillet and cook over medium-low heat for 1 minute. Then stir in broccoli and 3 tablespoons of cheese. Remove from heat and let cool.
6. In a medium bowl, beat egg white substitute and cream of tartar with an electric mixer until stiff peaks form.
7. Gently fold ¼ egg whites into broccoli mixture; then fold in the remaining egg whites.
8. Coat a 1½-quart soufflé dish with cooking spray. Spoon broccoli mixture into dish and sprinkle with remaining cheese.
9. Place dish in oven, reduce temperature to 375°F, and bake for 40 minutes until puffy and set. Serve immediately. Add salt and pepper to taste.

MAKES 4 SERVINGS

SERVING GUIDELINES

▶ **FOR LAP-BAND:**
   Weeks 1–4: Not recommended.
   Weeks 5+: Serve ¼–½ cup
      broccoli soufflé as is.

▶ **FOR BYPASS:**
   Weeks 1–4: Not recommended.
   Weeks 5+: Serve ¼–½ cup
      broccoli soufflé as is.

▶ **FOR BPD-DS:**
   Weeks 1–4: Not recommended.
   Weeks 5+: Serve ¼–½ cup
      broccoli soufflé as is.

▶ **FOR OTHERS:**
   Serve 1 cup broccoli soufflé as
      is.

Calories: 135.27, **Protein:** 13.80g, **Fat:** 2.28g, **Carbohydrates:** 17.26g, **Cholesterol:** 4mg, **Fiber:** 2.88g, **Sodium:** 292.25mg

Garlicky Broccoli and Ricotta

THIS IS A GREAT ITALIAN PEASANT DISH—RICH, FILLING, AND IN OUR VERSION, LOW FAT. IT ALSO TASTES GOOD AT ROOM TEMPERATURE.

4 cups (1 bunch) broccoli,
    trimmed and separated into
    large spears
cooking spray
2 large cloves garlic, minced
1 cup fat-free ricotta cheese
1 teaspoon fresh ginger, grated
¼ teaspoon red pepper

1. Steam the broccoli until soft, about 10–15 minutes.
2. Coat a small nonstick skillet with cooking spray and sauté garlic over medium heat until barely golden.
3. Cut broccoli into 1-inch pieces; place broccoli, ricotta, garlic, and seasonings in food processor and pulse until combined.

MAKES 4 SERVINGS

SERVING GUIDELINES

▶ **FOR LAP-BAND:**
  Weeks 1–4: Not recommended.
  Weeks 5+: Serve ¼–½ cup
    broccoli–ricotta mixture as is.

▶ **FOR BYPASS:**
  Weeks 1–4: Not recommended.
  Weeks 5+: Serve ¼–½ cup
    broccoli–ricotta mixture as is.

▶ **FOR BPD-DS:**
  Weeks 1–4: Not recommended.
  Weeks 5+: Serve ½–1 cup
    broccoli–ricotta mixture as is.

▶ **FOR OTHERS:**
  Serve 1 cup broccoli–ricotta mixture as is.

Calories: 88.02, **Protein:** 12.76g, **Fat:** 0.58g, **Carbohydrates:** 12.45g, **Cholesterol:** 6mg, **Fiber:** 4.58g, **Sodium:** 70.85mg

Celery Root Puree

FINALLY, A DELICIOUS SUBSTITUTE FOR POTATOES—CELERY ROOT (ALSO CALLED CELERIAC). IT MAY LOOK HAIRY AND UGLY ON THE OUTSIDE, BUT THE INSIDE HAS THE TEXTURE AND VERSATILITY OF POTATOES, WITHOUT ALL THE CARBOHYDRATES. THE TASTE IS MILD WITH A SLIGHTLY SWEET CELERY FLAVOR.

3 cups celery root (2 celery root knobs), peeled and cut into 1-inch cubes
1½ cups skim milk
1 tablespoon light heart-healthy margarine (such as Benecol light or Smart Balance light)
salt and pepper to taste

1. In a heavy saucepan, bring celery root and milk to a boil. Turn down heat and simmer, uncovered, for 30–40 minutes, until celery root is very soft.
2. With a slotted spoon, transfer celery root to a food processor and puree until smooth. Reserve milk mixture.
3. Add ½ cup of hot milk mixture and margarine and puree until well blended. Add salt and pepper to taste.

MAKES 4 SERVINGS

SERVING GUIDELINES

▶ **FOR LAP-BAND:**
Weeks 1–4: Not recommended.
Weeks 5+: Serve ¼–½ cup as is.

▶ **FOR BYPASS:**
Weeks 1–4: Not recommended.
Weeks 5+: Serve ¼–½ cup as is.

▶ **FOR BPD:**
Weeks 1–4: Not recommended.
Weeks 5+: Serve ¼–½ cup as is.

▶ **FOR OTHERS:**
Serve 1 cup as is.

Calories: 100.59, **Protein:** 6.19g, **Fat:** 3.18g, **Carbohydrates:** 11.43g, **Cholesterol:** 1.84mg, **Fiber:** 7.14g, **Sodium:** 105.55mg

Cauliflower, Mushroom, and Cheddar Casserole

TO ME, THIS IS ONE OF THOSE QUINTESSENTIAL WINTER DISHES—SOFT, PALE, AND RICH WITH FLAVOR. OF COURSE, I SPIFFED IT UP A BIT WITH ROASTED GARLIC AND THE CRUNCH OF A SOY NUT TOPPING.

3 cups cauliflower, steamed till soft, about 12 minutes
1 cup fresh white mushrooms, chopped
5 cloves roasted garlic
½ pound low-fat cheddar cheese, diced
butter-flavored cooking spray
2 tablespoons ground soy nuts

1. Preheat oven to 350°F.
2. In a large bowl, mix cauliflower, mushrooms, roasted garlic, and cheese.
3. Coat a small nonstick baking dish with cooking spray; pour in cauliflower mixture and sprinkle ground soy nuts on top.
4. Spray top with cooking spray and bake for 30 minutes.

MAKES 4 SERVINGS

▷ **COOKING TIP:** To roast garlic, take whole unpeeled head of garlic and cut off top, or however many cloves you need. Drizzle with 1 teaspoon olive oil, wrap in foil, and bake at 275°F for 1½–2 hours. Can be stored in refrigerator for up to one week.

SERVING GUIDELINES

▶ **FOR LAP-BAND:**
Weeks 1–4: Not recommended.
Weeks 5+: Serve ¼–½ cup as is.

▶ **FOR BYPASS:**
Weeks 1–4: Not recommended.
Weeks 5+: Serve ¼–½ cup as is.

▶ **FOR BPD-DS:**
Weeks 1–4: Not recommended.
Weeks 5+: Serve ½–1 cup as is.

▶ **FOR OTHERS:**
Serve 1 cup as is.

Calories: 151.96, **Protein:** 17.90g, **Fat:** 5.58g, **Carbohydrates:** 8.73g, **Cholesterol:** 11.88mg, **Fiber:** 3.11g, **Sodium:** 370.44mg

Mashed Cauliflower

OKAY, SO IT'S NOT MASHED POTATOES, BUT IT IS DELICIOUS—SMOOTH AND SOFT AND BUTTERY-TASTING, WITHOUT ALL THE CALORIES AND CARBS.

3 cups cauliflower florets
⅔ cup skim milk
4 tablespoons fat-free sour cream
salt and pepper to taste
20 sprays (5 per person) artificial refrigerated butter spray (I Can't Believe It's Not Butter works well)

1. Place cauliflower in a steamer insert in a 4-quart pot, cover, and steam for 10–15 minutes until very soft.
2. Place cooked cauliflower florets in food processor and puree.
3. Add milk, sour cream, salt, and pepper to cauliflower and puree until smooth.
4. Put mixture in microwave-safe dish and heat for 2 minutes; spray with butter spray.

MAKES 4 SERVINGS

SERVING GUIDELINES

▶ **FOR LAP-BAND:**
  Weeks 1–4: Not recommended.
  Weeks 5+: Serve ¼–½ cup as is.

▶ **FOR BYPASS:**
  Weeks 1–4: Not recommended.
  Weeks 5+: Serve ¼–½ cup as is.

▶ **FOR BPD:**
  Weeks 1–4: Not recommended.
  Weeks 5+: Serve ¼–½ cup as is.

▶ **FOR OTHERS:**
  Serve 1 cup as is.

Calories: 202.17, **Protein:** 15.51g, **Fat:** 0.92g, **Carbohydrates:** 35.52g, **Cholesterol:** 13.27mg, **Fiber:** 7.50g, **Sodium:** 224.93mg

Creamed Spinach

AT LAST, A LOW-FAT VERSION OF EVERYONE'S FAVORITE SIDE DISH. IT TASTES AS RICH AND CREAMY AS THE ORIGINAL.

1 10-ounce package frozen
  chopped spinach, defrosted
cooking spray
¼ cup shallot, sliced thin
⅓ cup skim milk
½ cup fat-free cream cheese
¼ teaspoon ground nutmeg
  (optional)
salt and pepper to taste

1. Place defrosted spinach in 2 layers of paper towels and squeeze to remove as much liquid as possible.
2. Coat saucepan with cooking spray and place over medium heat until hot.
3. Add the shallots and sauté until lightly browned.
4. Reduce heat and add milk, cream cheese, and nutmeg and whisk until smooth.
5. Stir in spinach, cover pan, and simmer for 10 minutes. Remove the cover, raise heat to medium, and cook for 1 minute more. Add salt and pepper to taste.

MAKES 4 SERVINGS

SERVING GUIDELINES

▶ **FOR LAP-BAND:**
   Weeks 1–4: Not recommended.
   Weeks 5+: Serve ¼–½ cup as is.

▶ **FOR BYPASS:**
   Weeks 1–4: Not recommended.
   Weeks 5+: Serve ¼–½ cup as is.

▶ **FOR BPD**
   Weeks 1–4: Not recommended.
   Weeks 4+: Serve ¼–½ cup as is.

▶ **FOR OTHERS:**
   Serve ½ cup as is.

Calories: 61.74, **Protein:** 6.62g, **Fat:** 0.10g, **Carbohydrates:** 7.24g, **Cholesterol:** 5.41mg, **Fiber:** 2.53g, **Sodium:** 206.04mg

Crustless Spinach and Cheese Quiche

This is, without a doubt, one of my favorite vegetable dishes. It's a basic quiche—custard and cheese—that you don't always have to make with spinach (sometimes I use broccoli, asparagus, or zucchini). I've even been known to add diced red bell pepper. So go ahead, experiment—but remember, the nutritional numbers may change.

butter-flavored cooking spray

¾ cup fresh white mushrooms, chopped

¼ cup shallots, chopped

2 10-ounce packages frozen chopped spinach

1 tablespoon water

¼ cup egg substitute

½ cup skim milk

½ cup low-fat Swiss cheese, diced

¼ teaspoon ground nutmeg

1. Spray a microwaveable casserole dish with butter-flavored cooking spray. Add mushrooms and shallots, cover dish, and microwave on HIGH for 1 minute.
2. Place frozen spinach and water on top of mushroom mixture. Cover and microwave on HIGH for 3½ minutes.
3. Uncover and break up spinach, flipping it over. Re-cover and microwave on HIGH for another 3½ minutes. Remove from microwave and drain if too liquidy.
4. In a separate bowl, combine egg substitute and milk and stir in diced cheese and nutmeg.
5. Stir spinach, mushrooms, and shallots in casserole dish to combine. Pour egg-milk-cheese mixture on top, cover, and microwave on HIGH for 4 minutes.

Makes 4 servings

SERVING GUIDELINES

▶ **FOR LAP-BAND:**
Weeks 1–4: Not recommended.
Weeks 5+: Serve ¼–½ cup as is.

▶ **FOR BYPASS:**
Weeks 1–4: Not recommended.
Weeks 5+: Serve ¼–½ cup as is.

▶ **FOR BPD-DS:**
Weeks 1–4: Not recommended.
Weeks 4+: Serve ½–1 cup as is.

▶ **FOR OTHERS:**
Serve 1 cup as is.

Calories: 142.77, **Protein:** 15.52g, **Fat:** 4.16g, **Carbohydrates:** 10.02g, **Cholesterol:** 15.61mg, **Fiber:** 5.19g, **Sodium:** 221.07mg

Kale with Apples and Onions

Unlike most of the other vegetable dishes in this book, this one has no protein, so it really is only a side dish. I love to serve it with most of the pork recipes we've created. We adapted this recipe from *Gourmet* magazine.

1 medium Granny Smith apple
  (¼ pound), peeled and cored
olive oil cooking spray
¾ cup chopped onion
⅛ teaspoon curry powder
4 cups (1 bunch) kale, tough
  stems and ribs removed,
  coarsely chopped
½ cup water

1. Cut apple into wedges, then into ¼-inch slices.
2. Coat 4- to 5-quart nonstick pot with cooking spray and heat over medium-high heat until hot but not smoking. Sauté the onion, stirring occasionally, until golden.
3. Stir in apple and curry powder, reduce heat, cover pot, and cook for 2 minutes until apple is almost tender.
4. Add kale and water and cook, covered, about 5 minutes until kale is tender and most of liquid has evaporated.

Makes 4 servings

SERVING GUIDELINES

▶ **FOR LAP-BAND:**
  Weeks 1–4: Not recommended.
  Weeks 5+: Serve ¼ cup
    kale–apple mixture as is.

▶ **FOR BYPASS:**
  Weeks 1–4: Not recommended.
  Weeks 5+: Serve ¼ cup
    kale–apple mixture as is.

▶ **FOR BPD-DS:**
  Weeks 1–3: Not recommended
  Weeks 4+: Serve ¼ cup
    kale–apple mixture as is.

▶ **FOR OTHERS:**
  Serve ½ cup kale–apple mixture
    as is.

Calories: 65.46, **Protein:** 2.63g, **Fat:** 0.65g, **Carbohydrates:** 14.59g, **Cholesterol:** 0mg, **Fiber:** 2.83g, **Sodium:** 29.74mg

Marinated String Beans

ANOTHER PURELY SIDE DISH VEGETABLE RECIPE (NO PROTEIN). I ALWAYS THINK OF THIS RECIPE AS PERFECT SUMMER FOOD—GREAT ON A PICNIC. YOU CAN SERVE IT HOT ALONG-SIDE BEEF OR LAMB, OR SERVE IT COLD AS A SUBSTITUTE FOR COLESLAW.

½ pound string beans, tips cut off

2 cups tomatoes, seeded and diced

5 cloves of garlic, peeled and cut in half horizontally

1 tablespoon dried basil

¼ cup water

2 teaspoons olive oil

1 tablespoon balsamic vinegar

salt and freshly ground pepper to taste

1. In a medium microwave-safe bowl, combine beans, tomatoes, garlic, basil, and water.
2. Cover and microwave on HIGH for 9 minutes until beans are soft.
3. Let bean mixture cool and then toss with oil, vinegar, salt, and pepper.
4. Serve it hot or cold (if you don't like a strong garlic flavor, remove garlic before serving).

MAKES 4 SERVINGS

SERVING GUIDELINES

▶ **FOR LAP-BAND:**
Weeks 1–4: Not recommended.
Weeks 5+: Serve ¼ cup as is.

▶ **FOR BYPASS:**
Weeks 1–4: Not recommended.
Weeks 5+: Serve ¼ cup as is.

▶ **FOR BPD-DS:**
Weeks 1–4: Not recommended.
Weeks 5+: Serve ¼ cup as is.

▶ **FOR OTHERS:**
Serve ½ cup as is.

Calories: 58.41, **Protein:** 1.49g, **Fat:** 2.66g, **Carbohydrates:** 8.32g, **Cholesterol:** 0mg, **Fiber:** 2.03g, **Sodium:** 249.02mg

Minted Cucumbers with Yogurt

You'll find a version of this recipe in Indian cooking as well as in Middle Eastern and Greek cuisines. It's very refreshing, especially when served with spicy dishes. Use it in a chunky state as a side dish, or puree it and serve as a sauce over fish or grilled lamb.

3 cups (2 large) cucumbers, peeled and seeded

1 cup plain, fat-free yogurt

1 clove garlic, peeled and quartered

2 teaspoons lemon juice

½ teaspoon cumin

2 teaspoons fresh mint or 1 teaspoon dried mint

1. Dice cucumbers.
2. Combine all ingredients except cucumbers in food processor and process until smooth.
3. In a large bowl, toss cucumbers with yogurt mixture.

Serves 4

SERVING GUIDELINES

▶ **FOR LAP-BAND:**
Weeks 1–4: Not recommended.
Weeks 5+: Serve ¼–½ cup as is.

▶ **FOR BYPASS:**
Weeks 1–4: Not recommended.
Weeks 5+: Serve ¼–½ cup as is.

▶ **FOR BPD-DS:**
Weeks 1–4: Not recommended.
Weeks 5+: Serve ½–1 cup as is.

▶ **FOR OTHERS:**
Serve 1 cup as is.

Calories: 68.20, **Protein:** 5.19g, **Fat:** 0.35g, **Carbohydrates:** 11.46g, **Cholesterol:** 1.67mg, **Fiber:** 1.67g, **Sodium:** 69.08mg

Pattypan Squash Puree

IF YOU'VE NEVER TRIED THESE DELICATE LITTLE VEGGIES, YOU'VE MISSED OUT. THIS PUREE IS AS ELEGANT AS ANYTHING YOU'LL FIND IN FINE RESTAURANTS, AND IT'S REALLY FUN TO WATCH FRIENDS AND FAMILY GUESS WHAT'S IN IT.

3 cups green baby pattypan squash, cut in half, stems removed

¼ cup shallots (2), peeled and cut in half

½ cup fat-free sour cream

½ cup fat-free cream cheese

1 tablespoon prepared horse-radish

½ teaspoon dried thyme

salt and pepper to taste

1. Place squash and shallots in steamer basket in covered saucepan and steam over medium heat for 15 minutes until soft.
2. Remove squash and shallots from pan and place in food processor. Add sour cream, cream cheese, horseradish, and thyme and process until smooth. Add salt and pepper to taste.

MAKES 4 SERVINGS

SERVING GUIDELINES

▶ **FOR LAP-BAND:**
Weeks 1–4: Not recommended.
Weeks 5+: Serve ¼–½ cup as is.

▶ **FOR BYPASS:**
Weeks 1–4: Not recommended.
Weeks 5+: Serve ¼–½ cup as is.

▶ **FOR BPD-DS:**
Weeks 1–4: Not recommended.
Weeks 5+: Serve ¼–½ cup as is.

▶ **FOR OTHERS:**
Serve 1 cup as is.

Calories: 103.30, **Protein:** 8g, **Fat:** 0.77g, **Carbohydrates:** 15.96g, **Cholesterol:** 10mg, **Fiber:** 1.55g, **Sodium:** 210.95mg

Zucchini and Ricotta Rustica

The Italians have a delicious dish called Torta Rustica, a pie filled with cheeses, vegetables, and fresh herbs. We've taken it out of the pie crust and added some Canadian bacon for a slightly smoky flavor.

olive oil cooking spray

3 cups (2 medium) zucchini, sliced thin

salt and pepper to taste

½ pound Canadian bacon, sliced thin, trimmed of fat and diced

1½ cups fresh tomato, diced

½ cup fresh basil, shredded

½ cup fat-free ricotta cheese

2 tablespoons grated Parmesan cheese

1. In a large nonstick skillet, heat cooking spray until hot but not smoking. Add the zucchini, season with salt and pepper, and sauté over moderate heat until softened.
2. Stir in the Canadian bacon, tomato, and basil and cook until tomato is softened.
3. Remove from heat and toss with the ricotta and Parmesan cheeses.

Makes 4 servings

SERVING GUIDELINES

▶ **FOR LAP-BAND:**
Weeks 1–4: Not recommended.
Weeks 5+: Serve ¼–½ cup as is.

▶ **FOR BYPASS:**
Weeks 1–4: Not recommended
Weeks 5+: Serve ¼–½ cup as is.

▶ **FOR BDP-DS:**
Weeks 1–4: Not recommended.
Weeks 5+: Serve ½–1 cup as is.

▶ **FOR OTHERS:**
Serve 1 cup as is.

Calories: 150.13, **Protein:** 18.79g, **Fat:** 5.38g, **Carbohydrates:** 8.56g, **Cholesterol:** 5mg, **Fiber:** 2.07g, **Sodium:** 701.58mg

Zucchini Flan with Quick Tomato Sauce

A PERFECT RECIPE FOR WEEKEND BRUNCH OR A LIGHT DINNER. YOU'LL PROBABLY HAVE SOME TOMATO SAUCE LEFT OVER—I SAVE IT TO USE ON CHICKEN OR FISH. YOU CAN EVEN FREEZE THE LEFTOVER SAUCE IN ICE CUBE TRAYS TO DEFROST AND USE LATER.

cooking spray
4 cups zucchini, sliced thin
1 tablespoon garlic, minced
½ cup onion, sliced thin
1 cup egg substitute
¼ cup skim milk

Quick Tomato Sauce
   (makes approximately 1 cup):
olive oil cooking spray
1 clove garlic, minced
1 14.5-ounce can diced
   tomatoes
2 tablespoons fresh basil leaves,
   chopped
1 packet artificial sweetener
   (Splenda or Sweet 'N Low)
salt and pepper to taste

1. Preheat oven to 350°F.
2. *To make flan*: Coat a large nonstick skillet with cooking spray, add zucchini, and sauté over medium heat for about 10 minutes, stirring occasionally, until zucchini wilts and gives up its liquid.
3. Add garlic and onion and continue to cook until zucchini browns slightly. Turn off heat and let cool.
4. In a large bowl, beat together egg substitute and milk. Add zucchini mixture to eggs.
5. Coat an 8½ x ½-inch loaf pan with cooking spray and pour zucchini-egg mixture into it.
6. Place loaf pan in a baking dish and pour hot water around loaf pan until baking dish is as full as possible without getting water into the loaf pan. Bake until flan is set, but still wobbly in middle, about 30 minutes. Remove from oven and cool on rack for about 5 minutes.
7. While flan is baking, make sauce. Coat a small saucepan with cooking spray and brown garlic for 1 minute. Stir in tomatoes, basil, and sweetener and simmer for 5–7 minutes.
8. Invert loaf pan over a plate and unmold flan; then slice.

MAKES 4 SERVINGS

ZUCCHINI FLAN:
    Calories: 70.88, **Protein:** 8.64g, **Fat:** 0.28g, **Carbohydrates:** 9.40g,
    Cholesterol: 0.31mg, **Fiber:** 1.99g, **Sodium:** 113.49mg

QUICK TOMATO SAUCE (2 TABLESPOONS):
    Calories: 8.50, **Protein:** 0.43g, **Fat:** 0g, **Carbohydrates:** 1.73g,
    Cholesterol: 0mg, **Fiber:** 0.42g, **Sodium:** 38.68mg

SERVING GUIDELINES

▶ **FOR LAP-BAND:**
    Weeks 1–4: Puree ¼–½ cup flan
    with 2 tablespoons sauce until
    smooth.
    Weeks 5+: Serve ¼–½ cup flan
    topped with 2 tablespoons
    sauce.

▶ **FOR BYPASS:**
    Weeks 1–4: Puree ¼–½ cup flan
    with 2 tablespoons sauce until
    smooth.
    Weeks 5+: Serve ¼–½ cup flan
    topped with 2 tablespoons
    sauce.

▶ **FOR BPD-DS:**
    Weeks 1–3: Puree ¼–½ cup flan
    with 2 tablespoons sauce until
    smooth.
    Weeks 4+: Serve ½–1 cup flan
    topped with 2 tablespoons
    sauce.

▶ **FOR OTHERS:**
    Serve 1 cup flan with 2 table-
    spoons sauce.

Zucchini Custards

These are dainty little custards that look simply lovely on a plate—almost as delicate as a soufflé, but extremely flavorful. I usually serve them with lamb or fish.

3 cups zucchini, grated
cooking spray
¼ cup shallot, minced
½ cup egg substitute
3 tablespoons egg white
  substitute
¾ cup skim milk
1½ tablespoons dried basil
1 teaspoon dried oregano
¼ teaspoon ground nutmeg
⅛ teaspoon ground red pepper
salt and pepper to taste
3 tablespoons grated Parmesan
  cheese

1. Preheat oven to 350°F.
2. Spread grated zucchini on 2 layers of paper towels, cover with additional paper towels, and let stand 15 minutes, pressing occasionally until barely moist.
3. Coat the bottom of a small nonstick skillet with cooking spray and sauté shallots until lightly browned.
4. In the container of your food processor, combine egg substitute, egg white substitute, milk, and seasonings and process until well blended.
5. Add zucchini, cheese, and shallots and pulse until combined.
6. Coat 8 small (4-ounce) ramekins with cooking spray and spoon zucchini mixture into cups. Place ramekins into baking pan and pour about 1 inch of hot water into the pan. Be careful not to spill any water into the ramekins. Bake for 40 minutes.
7. Serve in ramekins or run knife around inside edges of ramekins and invert onto plates.

Makes 8 servings

SERVING GUIDELINES

▶ **FOR LAP-BAND:**
  Weeks 1+: Serve 1 custard as is.

▶ **FOR BYPASS:**
  Weeks 1+: Serve 1 custard as is.

▶ **FOR BDP-DS:**
  Weeks 1+: Serve 1 custard as is.

▶ **FOR OTHERS:**
  Serve 1 custard as is.

Calories: 38.33, **Protein:** 4.30g, **Fat:** 0.90g, **Carbohydrates:** 4.20g, **Cholesterol:** 1.96mg, **Fiber:** 0.61g, **Sodium:** 84.09mg

Zucchini Pancakes

These are such fun—light and delicate, fresh and green. You can serve them at breakfast, brunch, lunch, or dinner. They're especially good as a side dish with fish.

4 cups grated zucchini, about
1 pound
¼ cup grated Parmesan cheese
¼ cup fresh basil, chopped
2 tablespoons fresh chives,
chopped
1 packet artificial sweetener
(Splenda or Sweet 'N Low)
6 tablespoons egg white
substitute
cooking spray
½ cup fat-free sour cream
salt and pepper to taste

1. Place grated zucchini in a colander, let stand for 20 minutes at room temperature, then wrap zucchini in 3 layers of paper towels, top with another 3 layers of towels, and wring out as much liquid as possible.
2. Place zucchini in a bowl and mix with cheese, basil, chives, and sweetener.
3. In a separate bowl, beat egg whites with an electric mixer until they hold stiff peaks, then gently fold into zucchini mixture.
4. Heat cooking spray in a 10-inch nonstick skillet over moderately high heat until hot but not smoking. Spoon 2 tablespoons of zucchini mixture per pancake into skillet (skillet should accommodate about 5 pancakes at a time), flattening slightly, and sauté 3 minutes each side, turning once, until golden brown.
5. Remove cooked pancakes to plate and keep warm. Re-spray skillet and repeat cooking steps until all pancakes are cooked.
6. Top with fat-free sour cream and add salt and pepper to taste.

Makes 4 servings (16 pancakes)

SERVING GUIDELINES

▶ **FOR LAP-BAND:**
Weeks 1–4: Not recommended.
Weeks 5+: Serve 1–2 pancakes with 2 tablespoons sour cream.

▶ **FOR BYPASS:**
Weeks 1–4: Not recommended.
Weeks 5+: Serve 1–2 pancakes with 2 tablespoons sour cream

▶ **FOR BPD-DS:**
Weeks 1–4: Not recommended.
Weeks 5+: Serve 2–4 pancakes with 2 tablespoons sour cream.

▶ **FOR OTHERS:**
Serve 4 pancakes with 2 tablespoons sour cream.

Calories: 88.53, **Protein:** 7.76g, **Fat:** 2.19g, **Carbohydrates:** 11.34g, **Cholesterol:** 9mg, **Fiber:** 1.59g, **Sodium:** 161.33mg

Main Course

THIS IS REALLY the meat (pardon the pun) of any cookbook. We've created recipes that give you an incredible variety of flavors, textures, ethnic influences, and cooking styles. That's because Michele and I know that there's nothing more boring than an eating program that depends on one small group of ingredients or just relegates you to broiling and baking your food.

Every recipe has been developed to taste great in whatever form you're eating it—pureed, chopped, or as cooked. You'll find elegant quick sautés and succulent slow-cooked stews. There are spicy marinated dishes and taste bud–tingling curries. There's an exotic *tagine* from Morocco as well as a tropical seafood salad from the Caribbean. You can even make Italian-style lasagna, using our two luscious pasta-free recipes. And, of course, we've included a number of delectably simple American dishes.

Every recipe is protein rich, low fat, and has no "bad" carbohydrates. We use lean cuts of meat, skinless poultry, and lots of different fish and shellfish, plus tofu and low-fat or fat-free cheeses.

There are a lot of cooking tricks out there involving ingredients and techniques that can be used to make sure you don't feel deprived, but it takes time and experimentation to figure them out. You don't have to do it—we did it for you. For instance, once you're past your soft-food period, we teach you how to add crunch to a dish by topping it with ground soy

Meat, poultry, seafood, and vegetarian entrées to please your palate

nuts—a great source of protein. We'll even show you how to use them to bread cutlets that are "fried" using cooking spray.

Of course, the greatest reward after having weight reduction surgery is achieving your weight loss goals. But along the way, this cookbook will make each meal a reward in itself.

Note: The nutritional analyses are based on an average portion size (*Others'* portions).

BBQ-Baked Chicken

THIS IS FOR PEOPLE WHO LIKE REALLY TANGY BARBECUE SAUCE. THIS CHICKEN ALSO TASTES GREAT SERVED COLD.

½ cup apple cider
¼ cup tomato paste
brown-sugar artificial sweetener (1 teaspoon measure)
1 tablespoon cider vinegar
1 teaspoon dried thyme
½ teaspoon Asian chili paste with garlic
1 pound skinless, boneless chicken thighs
cooking spray

1. Preheat oven to 350°F.
2. In a small bowl, combine first 6 ingredients and stir well.
3. Reserve ¼ cup and place remaining marinade and chicken in large zip-top plastic bag. Shake to coat, then refrigerate for 1 hour.
4. Remove chicken from bag and place in a nonstick baking pan that has been coated with cooking spray.
5. Bake chicken for 45 minutes until juices run clear when pierced with a fork. Remove chicken from pan and keep warm.
6. Skim any fat from pan juices and discard. Pour skimmed pan juices into a small saucepan and add reserved ¼ cup marinade. Stir over low heat for 2 minutes.

MAKES 4 SERVINGS

SERVING GUIDELINES

▶ **FOR LAP-BAND:**
Weeks 1–4: Puree 2 ounces cooked chicken with 2 tablespoons sauce.
Weeks 5–8: Chop 2 ounces cooked chicken and top with sauce.
Weeks 9+: Serve 2–4 ounces cooked chicken topped with sauce.

▶ **FOR BYPASS:**
Weeks 1–4: Puree 2 ounces cooked chicken with 2 tablespoons sauce.
Weeks 5–8: Chop 2 ounces cooked chicken and top with sauce.
Weeks 9+: Serve 2–4 ounces cooked chicken topped with sauce.

▶ **FOR BPD-DS:**
Weeks 1–3: Puree 3–4 ounces cooked chicken with 2 tablespoons sauce.
Weeks 5+: Serve 3–4 ounces cooked chicken topped with sauce.

▶ **FOR OTHERS:**
Serve 4 ounces cooked chicken topped with sauce.

Calories: 164.32, **Protein:** 23.48g, **Fat:** 4.60g, **Carbohydrates:** 6.67g, **Cholesterol:** 94.12mg, **Fiber:** 0.65g, **Sodium:** 117.78mg

Chicken and Fresh Apricot Tagine

THIS IS ONE OF THE MOST DELECTABLE CHICKEN RECIPES I KNOW, AND ACCORDING TO PEOPLE WHO HAVE SPENT TIME IN THE MIDDLE EAST, VERY AUTHENTIC. YOU CAN SUB-STITUTE WATER-PACKED CANNED APRICOTS, BUT I PREFER TO WAIT UNTIL FRESH ONES ARE IN SEASON.

cooking spray

salt and freshly ground pepper to taste

1 pound skinless, boneless chicken thighs

1 pound skinless, boneless chicken breasts, quartered

2 cups yellow onion, sliced thin

1 large clove garlic, minced

1½ pounds (10–12) small ripe apricots, quartered and pitted

1½ teaspoons cinnamon

¼ teaspoon ground ginger

¼ teaspoon ground coriander

¼ teaspoon saffron threads

⅔ cup fat-free, low-sodium chicken broth

6 packets artificial sweetener (Splenda or Sweet 'N Low)

1. In a cooking pot large enough to hold all the pieces of chicken in one layer, heat cooking spray till hot but not smoking.
2. Salt and pepper chicken and brown in pot for about 4 minutes on each side. Remove chicken to a paper towel-lined plate.
3. Add onion to pot and cook, stirring occasionally, for 5 minutes until lightly browned.
4. Add garlic and sauté for 1 minute. Stir in apricots, cinnamon, ginger, coriander, saffron, broth, and sweetener.
5. Place chicken on top of apricot mixture and cover. Reduce heat to low and cook for 45–50 minutes, or until chicken is cooked through and sauce is thickened.
6. If sauce has not thickened at end of cooking time, remove chicken to preheated 200°F oven to keep warm. Reduce sauce, uncovered, over medium flame until thick.

MAKES 8 SERVINGS

Calories: 296.49, **Protein:** 29.12g, **Fat:** 4.25g, **Carbohydrates:** 39.56g, **Cholesterol:** 79.95mg, **Fiber:** 8.90g, **Sodium:** 147.15mg

SERVING GUIDELINES

▶ **FOR LAP-BAND:**
Weeks 1–4: Puree 2 ounces cooked chicken with 2 tablespoons apricot sauce.
Weeks 5–8: Chop 2 ounces cooked chicken and top with apricot sauce.
Weeks 9+: Serve 2–4 ounces cooked chicken topped with apricot sauce.

▶ **FOR BYPASS:**
Weeks 1–4: Puree 2 ounces cooked chicken with 2 tablespoons apricot sauce.
Weeks 5–8: Chop 2 ounces cooked chicken and top with apricot sauce.
Weeks 9+: Serve 2–4 ounces cooked chicken topped with apricot sauce.

▶ **FOR BPD-DS:**
Weeks 1–3: Puree 2–3 ounces cooked chicken with 2 tablespoons apricot sauce.
Weeks 4+: Serve 3–4 ounces cooked chicken topped with apricot sauce.

▶ **FOR OTHERS:**
Serve 4 ounces cooked chicken topped with apricot sauce.

Chicken with Fresh Figs

I LOVE THE COMBINATION OF MEAT OR CHICKEN AND FRUIT. SO WHEN FRESH FIGS COME INTO SEASON, I IMMEDIATELY LOOK FOR NEW WAYS TO USE THEM. IN THIS RECIPE, THE BALSAMIC VINEGAR, CINNAMON, AND GINGER SEEM TO INTENSIFY THE FIG FLAVOR.

cooking spray
2 large shallots, chopped
1½ teaspoons fresh ginger, minced
1 pound chicken breast cutlets
½ cup white wine
1 tablespoon balsamic vinegar
1 tablespoon concentrated chicken broth
¼ cup water
¼ teaspoon cinnamon
brown-sugar artificial sweetener (1 teaspoon equivalent)
½ pound small black fresh figs, quartered

1. Coat a medium nonstick skillet with cooking spray. Over medium heat, lightly brown shallots. Add ginger and cook for 1 minute.
2. Remove shallots and ginger from pan. Place cutlets in pan and brown, about 1–2 minutes per side. Remove cutlets and de-glaze pan with wine, stirring to scrape up any brown bits.
3. Add balsamic vinegar, concentrated chicken broth, water, cinnamon, and brown sugar sweetener and simmer for 2 minutes.
4. Add in figs, shallots, and ginger and cook over low heat, stirring, for about 5 minutes until figs soften and sauce thickens.
5. Add chicken and any accumulated juices back to pan and turn to coat. Then cover the pan and cook for 1 minute.

MAKES 4 SERVINGS

SERVING GUIDELINES

▶ **FOR LAP-BAND:**
Weeks 1–4: Puree 2 ounces cooked cutlet with 2 tablespoons fig sauce.
Weeks 5–8: Chop 2 ounces cooked cutlet with fig sauce.
Weeks 9+: Serve 2–4 ounces cooked cutlet topped with fig sauce.

▶ **FOR BYPASS:**
Weeks 1–4: Puree 2 ounces cooked cutlet with 2 tablespoons of fig sauce.
Weeks 5–8: Chop 2 ounces cooked cutlet with fig sauce.
Weeks 9+: Serve 2–4 ounces cooked cutlet topped with fig sauce.

▶ **FOR BPD-DS:**
Weeks 1–3: Puree 2 ounces cooked cutlet with 2 tablespoons fig sauce.
Weeks 4+: Serve 3–4 ounces cooked cutlet topped with fig sauce.

▶ **FOR OTHERS:**
Serve 4 ounces cooked cutlet topped with fig sauce.

Calories: 213.96, **Protein:** 26.90g, **Fat:** 1.78g, **Carbohydrates:** 14.25g, **Cholesterol:** 65.77mg, **Fiber:** 1.89g, **Sodium:** 359.51mg

Chicken and Spinach Adobo

THIS IS AN ADAPTATION OF A CLASSIC FILIPINO RECIPE. IT'S GOT A LITTLE BIT OF A KICK FROM THE RED PEPPERS, WHICH SOME PEOPLE LIKE TO KICK HIGHER BY ADDING MORE.

¼ cup cider vinegar

¼ cup light soy sauce

1 clove garlic, minced

1 bay leaf

¼ teaspoon red pepper flakes

1 pound boneless, skinless
   chicken thighs

cooking spray

1 10-ounce package chopped
   frozen spinach, thawed

SERVING GUIDELINES

▶ **FOR LAP-BAND:**
   Weeks 1–4: Puree 2 ounces
   cooked chicken with 2 tablespoons spinach and sauce.
   Weeks 5–8: Chop 2 ounces
   cooked chicken and top with
   spinach and sauce.
   Week 9+: Serve 2–4 ounces
   cooked chicken topped with
   spinach and sauce.

▶ **FOR BYPASS:**
   Weeks 1–4: Puree 2 ounces
   cooked chicken with 2 tablespoons spinach and sauce.
   Weeks 5–8: Chop 2 ounces
   cooked chicken and top with
   spinach and sauce.
   Week 9+: Serve 2–4 ounces
   cooked chicken topped with
   spinach and sauce.

▶ **FOR BPD-DS:**
   Weeks 1–3: Puree 3–4 ounces
   cooked chicken with 2 tablespoons spinach and sauce.
   Week 4+: Serve 3–4 ounces
   cooked chicken topped with
   spinach and sauce.

▶ **FOR OTHERS:**
   Serve 4 ounces cooked chicken
   topped with spinach and sauce.

1. Mix together vinegar, soy sauce, garlic, bay leaf, and red pepper flakes in a bowl.
2. Pour into a zip-top plastic bag, add chicken, and turn bag to coat. Marinate in refrigerator for 2 hours, turning occasionally. Remove chicken from bag and reserve marinade.
3. Coat large nonstick skillet with cooking spray and sauté chicken over medium-high heat for 7 minutes, turning to brown evenly.
4. While chicken is browning, place spinach in 2 layers of paper towels and squeeze out moisture.
5. Remove chicken from pan. Then pour reserved marinade in pan and bring to a boil.
6. Stir in spinach and place chicken on top. Lower the heat, cover the pan, and cook for 10 minutes.
7. Remove chicken and keep warm. Raise heat to medium-high and reduce liquid by half, about 5–7 minutes.

MAKES 4 SERVINGS

Calories: 168.97, **Protein:** 25.65g, **Fat:** 4.51g, **Carbohydrates:** 5.08g, **Cholesterol:** 94.12mg, **Fiber:** 2.59g, **Sodium:** 693.92mg

Chicken Beau Sejour

ORIGINALLY, I MADE THIS RECIPE WITH VEAL. ONE DAY I HAD THE BRILLIANT IDEA TO TRY IT WITH CHICKEN AND HAVE MADE IT THAT WAY EVER SINCE. THE VINEGAR AND THYME ARE A CLASSIC FRENCH FLAVOR COMBINATION.

cooking spray

1 pound boneless, skinless chicken breast

2 teaspoons fresh thyme or 1 teaspoon dried thyme

2 bay leaves

4 large cloves of garlic, sliced in half horizontally

½ pound white mushrooms, sliced thick

2 tablespoons red-wine vinegar

½ cup fat-free, low-sodium chicken broth

salt and pepper to taste

1. In a large nonstick skillet, heat cooking spray; add chicken, brown on one side, then turn.
2. Sprinkle chicken with thyme and place 1 bay leaf on each piece. Arrange garlic, cut side down, around chicken and layer mushroom slices over garlic. Cover pan and cook over low heat for 15 minutes.
3. Remove chicken and mushrooms from pan, discard bay leaves, and keep warm.
4. De-glaze pan with vinegar and bring to a simmer, scraping up any brown bits. Add chicken broth to pan, press down on garlic to mash (if you don't want so pungent a garlic flavor, remove and discard garlic before adding broth).
5. Simmer broth for 2 minutes until slightly reduced. Add chicken and mushrooms and any chicken juices that have accumulated. Add salt and pepper to taste.

MAKES 4 SERVINGS

SERVING GUIDELINES

▶ FOR LAP-BAND:
Weeks 1–4: Puree 2 ounces chicken with 2 tablespoons mushroom sauce until smooth.
Weeks 5–8: Chop 2 ounces chicken and top with mushroom sauce.
Weeks 9+: Serve 2–4 ounces chicken with mushroom sauce.

▶ FOR BYPASS:
Weeks 1–4: Puree 2 ounces chicken with 2 tablespoons sauce until smooth.
Weeks 5–8: Chop 2 ounces chicken and top with mushroom sauce.
Weeks 9+: Serve 2–4 ounces chicken with mushroom sauce.

▶ FOR BPD-DS:
Weeks 1–3: Puree 2–3 ounces chicken with 2 tablespoons mushroom sauce until smooth.
Weeks 4+: Serve 3–4 ounces chicken with mushroom sauce.

▶ FOR OTHERS:
Serve 4 ounces chicken with mushroom sauce.

Calories: 146.58, **Protein:** 28.21g, **Fat:** 1.65g, **Carbohydrates:** 4.02g, **Cholesterol:** 65.77mg, **Fiber:** 0.92g, **Sodium:** 162.14mg

Chicken Breasts Stuffed with Ham and Cheese

WE'VE UPDATED A CLASSIC, MAKING IT LIGHTER AND, WE THINK, BETTER. WITH JUST A WHITE WINE AND MUSHROOM SAUCE INSTEAD OF A HEAVY CREAM SAUCE, YOU REALLY TASTE HOW WELL ALL THE FLAVORS COMPLEMENT ONE ANOTHER.

1 pound chicken breast cutlets, pounded very thin

4 ounces lean boiled ham, sliced thin (4 slices)

4 ounces low-fat Swiss cheese, sliced thin (4 slices)

cooking spray

1 cup fresh mushrooms, sliced thin

1 large shallot, finely minced

½ cup white wine

¼ cup fat-free, low-sodium chicken broth

1 teaspoon dried tarragon

salt and pepper to taste

1. Cut pounded chicken into 8 thin cutlets. Lay out 4 cutlets; top each with 1 slice of ham and 1 slice of cheese, and then top with a second cutlet.
2. Coat a large nonstick skillet with cooking spray and sauté layered chicken-ham-cheese over medium-high heat, carefully turning once, for 8–10 minutes, until golden and cooked through. Remove to a plate and keep warm.
3. Re-spray pan and sauté mushrooms and shallot over medium-high heat, stirring for 3 minutes. Add wine to de-glaze pan, stirring to scrape up any brown bits, until it's reduced by half.
4. Add chicken broth and tarragon and simmer for 2 minutes. Stir in any chicken juices that have accumulated on plate and add salt and pepper to taste.

MAKES 4 SERVINGS

SERVING GUIDELINES

▶ **FOR LAP-BAND:**
Weeks 1–4: Puree 2 ounces cooked chicken-ham-cheese with 2 tablespoons sauce.
Weeks 5–8: Chop 2 ounces cooked chicken-ham-cheese and top with sauce.
Weeks 9+: Serve 2–4 ounces cooked chicken-ham-cheese topped with sauce.

▶ **FOR BYPASS:**
Weeks 1–4: Puree 2 ounces cooked chicken-ham-cheese with 2 tablespoons sauce.
Weeks 5–8: Chop 2 ounces cooked chicken-ham-cheese and top with sauce.
Weeks 9+: Serve 2–4 ounces cooked chicken-ham-cheese topped with sauce.

▶ **FOR BPD-DS:**
Weeks 1–3: Puree 2–3 ounces cooked chicken-ham-cheese with 2 tablespoons sauce.
Weeks 4+: Serve 3–4 ounces cooked chicken-ham-cheese topped with sauce.

▶ **FOR OTHERS:**
Serve 4 ounces cooked chicken-ham-cheese topped with sauce.

Calories: 265.64, **Protein:** 40.71g, **Fat:** 6.40g, **Carbohydrates:** 4.23g, **Cholesterol:** 92.77mg, **Fiber:** 0.24g, **Sodium:** 434.49mg

Chicken Breasts with Creamy Tomato Sauce

TOO CREAMY TO BE A TOMATO SAUCE AND TOO LIGHT TO BE A CREAM SAUCE, THIS CREAMY TOMATO SAUCE IS A GREAT COMBINATION OF FLAVORS THAT TOPS OFF CHICKEN CUTLETS DELICIOUSLY.

cooking spray
1 pound chicken breast cutlets
½ pound fresh mushrooms,
  quartered
1 large shallot, finely minced
¼ cup white wine
½ cup canned diced tomatoes,
  drained
½ cup evaporated fat-free milk
salt and pepper to taste

SERVING GUIDELINES

▶ **FOR LAP-BAND:**
  Weeks 1–4: Puree 2 ounces cooked chicken with 2 tablespoons sauce.
  Weeks 5–8: Chop 2 ounces cooked chicken and top with sauce.
  Weeks 9+: Serve 2–4 ounces cooked chicken topped with sauce.

▶ **FOR BYPASS:**
  Weeks 1–4: Puree 2 ounces cooked chicken with 2 tablespoons sauce.
  Weeks 5–8: Chop 2 ounces cooked chicken and top with sauce.
  Weeks 9+: Serve 2–4 ounces cooked chicken topped with sauce.

▶ **FOR BPD-DS:**
  Weeks 1–3: Puree 2–3 ounces cooked chicken with 2 tablespoons sauce.
  Weeks 4+: Serve 3–4 ounces cooked chicken topped with sauce.

▶ **FOR OTHERS:**
  Serve 4 ounces cooked chicken topped with sauce.

1. Coat a large nonstick skillet with cooking spray and sauté chicken over medium-high heat for 3 minutes per side, until golden and cooked through. Remove chicken to a plate and keep warm.
2. Re-spray pan and sauté mushrooms and shallot over medium-high heat, stirring for 3 minutes. Add wine to de-glaze pan, stirring to scrape up any brown bits, until it's reduced by half. Add tomatoes and cook, stirring occasionally, for 3–4 minutes.
3. Reduce heat to low and add evaporated milk, stirring constantly, for 6–8 minutes until reduced by half. Stir in any chicken juices that have accumulated on plate and add salt and pepper to taste.

MAKES 4 SERVINGS

Calories: 187.55, **Protein:** 30.47g, **Fat:** 1.60g, **Carbohydrates:** 9.27g, **Cholesterol:** 65.77mg, **Fiber:** 1.18g, **Sodium:** 164.82mg

Chicken Sauté with Mushrooms

My mother used to tease me that I bought mushrooms the way most people bought bread and milk. This recipe really highlights the earthy taste of the mushrooms in a light creamy, tarragon-scented sauce.

olive oil cooking spray
1 pound chicken breast cutlets
3 tablespoons shallots, finely chopped
2 cups fresh mushrooms, sliced
½ cup white wine
¾ cup fat-free, low-sodium chicken broth
½ cup plain, fat-free yogurt
½ packet artificial sweetener (Splenda or Sweet 'N Low)
1 tablespoon fresh tarragon, finely chopped
salt and pepper to taste

1. In a large nonstick skillet, heat cooking spray until hot but not smoking. Sauté chicken for 3 minutes on each side until golden brown and no longer pink inside. Remove chicken from pan and keep warm.

2. Re-spray pan, add shallots and mushrooms, and cook, stirring, for about 2 minutes or until tender. Pour in wine, increase heat to high, and cook for 2 minutes.

3. Add broth and cook for 3–5 minutes, until reduced by half. Reduce heat to low and stir in yogurt and sweetener. Cook for about 2 minutes or until thick enough to coat spoon.

4. Stir in tarragon and season with salt and pepper to taste.

MAKES 4 SERVINGS

SERVING GUIDELINES

▶ **FOR LAP-BAND:**
Weeks 1–4: Puree 2 ounces cooked chicken with mushrooms and 2 tablespoons sauce.
Weeks 5–8: Chop 2 ounces cooked chicken and top with mushrooms and sauce.
Weeks 9+: Serve 2–4 ounces cooked chicken with mushrooms and sauce.

▶ **FOR BYPASS:**
Weeks 1–4: Puree 2 ounces cooked chicken with mushrooms and 2 tablespoons sauce.
Weeks 5–8: Chop 2 ounces cooked chicken and top with mushrooms and sauce.
Weeks 9+: Serve 2–4 ounces cooked chicken with mushrooms and sauce.

▶ **FOR BPD-DS:**
Weeks 1–3: Puree 2 ounces cooked chicken with mushrooms and 2 tablespoons sauce.
Weeks 4+: Serve 3–4 ounces cooked chicken topped with mushrooms and sauce.

▶ **FOR OTHERS:**
Serve 4 ounces cooked chicken with mushrooms and sauce.

Calories: 180.81, **Protein:** 29.40g, **Fat:** 1.61g, **Carbohydrates:** 6.44g, **Cholesterol:** 66.40mg, **Fiber:** 0.51g, **Sodium:** 230.26mg

Chicken with Oriental Mushrooms

THIS IS AN ASIAN-INFLUENCED RECIPE WITH A DECIDEDLY JAPANESE ACCENT. WITH ALL OF THE DIFFERENT TYPES OF MUSHROOMS AVAILABLE TODAY, I USE A DIFFERENT COMBINATION EVERY TIME I MAKE THIS DISH.

cooking spray
1 pound skinless, boneless
*   chicken breast cutlets*
1 garlic clove, minced
1½ cups fresh oyster mush-
*   rooms, sliced thin*
1½ cups white mushrooms,
*   sliced thin*
½ cup shiitake mushrooms,
*   sliced thin*
½ cup fat-free, low-sodium
*   chicken broth*
1 tablespoon rice vinegar
1 packet artificial sweetener
*   (Splenda or Sweet 'N Low)*
1½ teaspoons light soy sauce

1. In a large nonstick skillet, heat cooking spray until hot but not smoking. Add chicken cutlets and brown for 2 minutes on each side, then remove and keep warm.
2. Re-spray skillet, add garlic and mushrooms, and cook over medium heat, stirring, for 2–3 minutes until softened.
3. Stir in broth, vinegar, sweetener, and soy sauce and simmer, uncovered, for 4 minutes until mushrooms are tender.
4. Add chicken and any chicken juices that have accumulated. Turn cutlets to coat with sauce.

MAKES 4 SERVINGS

SERVING GUIDELINES

▶ **FOR LAP-BAND:**
   Weeks 1–4: Puree 2 ounces cooked chicken with mushrooms and 2 tablespoons sauce.
   Weeks 5–8: Chop 2 ounces cooked chicken and top with mushrooms and sauce.
   Weeks 9+: Serve 2–4 ounces cooked chicken topped with mushrooms and sauce.

▶ **FOR BYPASS:**
   Weeks 1–4: Puree 2 ounces cooked chicken with mushrooms and 2 tablespoons sauce.
   Weeks 5–8: Chop 2 ounces cooked chicken and top with mushrooms and sauce.
   Weeks 9+: Serve 2–4 ounces cooked chicken topped with mushrooms and sauce.

▶ **FOR BPD-DS:**
   Weeks 1–3: Puree 2–3 ounces cooked chicken with mushrooms and 2 tablespoons sauce.
   Weeks 4+: Serve 3–4 ounces cooked chicken topped with mushrooms and sauce.

▶ **FOR OTHERS:**
   Serve 4 ounces cooked chicken topped with mushrooms and sauce.

Calories: 182.29, **Protein:** 31.68g,
Fat: 1.99g, **Carbohydrates:** 10.71g,
Cholesterol: 65.77mg, **Fiber:** 2.75g,
Sodium: 435.91mg

Spicy Grilled Marinated Chicken Breasts

WE WERE LOOKING FOR A TASTY GRILLED CHICKEN RECIPE AND MICHELE CAME UP WITH THIS ONE. NOT ONLY DO THE CITRUS AND SPICES MAKE THE CHICKEN TANGY, THEY ACTUALLY MAKE IT MOUTH-MELTINGLY TENDER. YOU CAN ALSO MAKE THIS DISH IN THE BROILER.

Marinade:

½ cup low-fat sour cream

1 tablespoon freshly squeezed lime juice

2 tablespoons freshly squeezed orange juice

1 tablespoon freshly squeezed lemon juice

1 tablespoon chili powder

1 tablespoon paprika

½ teaspoon cayenne

⅛ teaspoon freshly ground pepper

2 tablespoons fresh tarragon

1 pound chicken breasts

cooking spray

1. Whisk marinade ingredients together and set aside.
2. Trim chicken of any fat and arrange in a shallow dish, just large enough to hold chicken in 1 layer. Add marinade (reserving 2 tablespoons) and toss to coat. Marinate chicken, covered, for 6–24 hours in refrigerator.
3. Prepare the grill.
4. Remove chicken from marinade; let excess drip off and discard.
5. Spray grill rack with cooking spray and grill chicken about 5 minutes on each side or until cooked through.

MAKES 4 SERVINGS

▷ **VARIATION:** If broiling, spray broiler pan with cooking spray, place chicken on pan, and broil about 5 minutes on each side or until cooked through.

SERVING GUIDELINES

▶ FOR LAP-BAND:
Weeks 1–4: Puree 2 ounces cooked chicken with 2 tablespoons reserved marinade.
Weeks 5–8: Chop 2 ounces cooked chicken.
Weeks 9+: Serve 2–4 ounces cooked chicken.

▶ FOR BYPASS:
Weeks 1–4: Puree 2 ounces cooked chicken with 2 tablespoons reserved marinade.
Weeks 5–8: Chop 2 ounces cooked chicken.
Weeks 9+: Serve 2–4 ounces cooked chicken.

▶ FOR BPD-DS:
Weeks 1–3: Puree 2 ounces cooked chicken with 2 tablespoons reserved marinade.
Weeks 4+: Serve 3–4 ounces cooked chicken.

▶ FOR OTHERS:
Serve 4 ounces cooked chicken.

Calories: 184.53, **Protein:** 29.32g, **Fat:** 2.17g, **Carbohydrates:** 10.87g, **Cholesterol:** 70.77mg, **Fiber:** 1.28g, **Sodium:** 119.96mg

Turkey Cutlets Francese

This has been one of my favorite recipes for years. By dipping the cutlets in egg and Parmesan, you don't miss the traditional breading at all.

½ cup grated Parmesan cheese
¼ cup dried parsley flakes
1 cup egg substitute
¼ cup skim milk
1 pound turkey cutlets, sliced
  thin
olive oil cooking spray
½ cup white wine
2 tablespoons concentrated
  chicken broth

1. On a flat plate, mix Parmesan cheese and parsley.
2. In a baking dish or platter with sides, mix eggs and milk. Dip cutlets into egg, then into cheese mixture, then back into egg.
3. Coat a nonstick skillet with cooking spray and heat until hot but not smoking. Sauté cutlets for 3 minutes on each side until brown. Remove to a plate and keep warm.
4. Reduce heat to low, pour wine into pan, and simmer, stirring to scrape up and brown bits.
5. Add concentrated chicken broth and continue simmering and stirring for 2 more minutes until sauce reduces slightly.

Makes 4 servings

SERVING GUIDELINES

▶ **FOR LAP-BAND:**
  Weeks 1–4: Puree 2 ounces cooked cutlet with 2 tablespoons sauce.
  Weeks 5–8: Chop 2 ounces cooked cutlet with 2 tablespoons sauce.
  Weeks 9+: Serve 2–4 ounces cooked cutlet topped with 2 tablespoons sauce.

▶ **FOR BYPASS:**
  Weeks 1–4: Puree 2 ounces cooked cutlet with 2 tablespoons sauce.
  Weeks 5–8: Chop 2 ounces cooked cutlet with 2 tablespoons sauce.
  Weeks 9+: Serve 2–4 ounces cooked cutlet topped with 2 tablespoons sauce.

▶ **FOR BPD-DS:**
  Weeks 1–3: Puree 2 ounces cooked cutlet with 2 tablespoons sauce.
  Weeks 4+: Serve 2–4 ounces cooked cutlet topped with 2 tablespoons sauce.

Calories: 255.08, **Protein:** 37.87g,
Fat: 6.47g, **Carbohydrates:** 6.53g,
Cholesterol: 76.35mg, **Fiber:** 0.30g,
Sodium: 838.88mg

▶ **FOR OTHERS**
  Serve 4 ounces cooked cutlet topped with 2 tablespoons sauce.

Turkey Cacciatore

THIS DISH IS JUST LIKE CHICKEN CACCIATORE, ONLY WE HAPPEN TO THINK IT'S BETTER. WAIT TILL YOU TASTE HOW THE DARK TURKEY MEAT STANDS UP TO THE GUTSY SOUTHERN ITALIAN FLAVORS.

olive oil cooking spray

1 pound skinless, boneless turkey thighs (or any dark turkey meat)

1 cup chopped onion

2 cloves garlic, minced

2 tablespoons sun-dried tomato paste

1 14.5-ounce can whole tomatoes

¼ cup fresh basil, chopped

1 teaspoon dried oregano

¼ teaspoon dried red pepper flakes

½ cup dry red wine

salt and pepper to taste

1. Heat cooking spray in a large nonstick cooking pot until hot but not smoking. Cook turkey for 3 minutes until browned all over and remove from pot.
2. Add onions and garlic and sauté for 2 minutes until lightly browned. Add tomato paste and cook, stirring until paste starts to darken.
3. Put turkey back in pot, add all other ingredients, and stir well.
4. Cover and reduce heat to low; simmer for 30 minutes until turkey is tender.

MAKES 4 SERVINGS

SERVING GUIDELINES

▶ **FOR LAP-BAND:**
Weeks 1–4: Puree 2 ounces turkey with 2 tablespoons sauce until smooth.
Weeks 5–8: Chop 2 ounces turkey and top with 2 tablespoons sauce.
Weeks 9+: Serve 2–4 ounces turkey topped with 2 tablespoons sauce.

▶ **FOR BYPASS:**
Weeks 1–4: Puree 2 ounces turkey with 2 tablespoons sauce until smooth.
Weeks 5–8: Chop 2 ounces turkey and top with 2 tablespoons sauce.
Weeks 9+: Serve 2–4 ounces turkey topped with 2 tablespoons sauce.

▶ **FOR BPD-DS:**
Weeks 1–3: Puree 2–3 ounces turkey with 2 tablespoons sauce until smooth.
Weeks 4+: Serve 2–4 ounces turkey with 2 tablespoons sauce.

▶ **FOR OTHERS:**
Serve 4 ounces turkey with 2 tablespoons sauce.

Calories: 224.19, **Protein:** 25.69g, **Fat:** 5.10g, **Carbohydrates:** 13.12g, **Cholesterol:** 78.25mg, **Fiber:** 2.87g, **Sodium:** 255.69mg

Turkey Paprikash

THIS IS AN UPDATED, LIGHTER VERSION OF A WELL-KNOWN HUNGARIAN CLASSIC.

cooking spray

1 pound boneless, skinless
   turkey thighs (or any dark
   turkey meat)

¼ cup chopped onion

1 garlic clove, minced

¼ pound (about 10) fresh
   mushrooms, sliced

1 tablespoon paprika

1½ teaspoons tomato paste

¼ teaspoon cayenne pepper

¼ cup fat-free, low-sodium
   chicken broth

2 tablespoons fat-free sour
   cream

salt to taste

1. Heat cooking spray in a medium skillet until hot but not smoking. Sauté turkey for 2 minutes to brown on each side.
2. Add onions and garlic, cover, lower heat, and cook for 10 minutes until turkey is cooked through. Remove turkey from pan and keep warm.
3. Stir in mushrooms, paprika, tomato paste, cayenne, and chicken broth into pan and cook, covered, for 3 minutes. Remove from heat and stir in sour cream and salt to taste.
4. Add turkey and turn to coat.

MAKES 4 SERVINGS

SERVING GUIDELINES

▶ **FOR LAP-BAND:**
   Weeks 1–4: Puree 2 ounces turkey with 2 tablespoons sauce until smooth.
   Weeks 5–8: Chop 2 ounces turkey and top with 2 tablespoons sauce.
   Weeks 9+: Serve 2–4 ounces turkey topped with 2 tablespoons sauce.

▶ **FOR BYPASS:**
   Weeks 1–4: Puree 2 ounces turkey with 2 tablespoons sauce until smooth.
   Weeks 5–8: Chop 2 ounces turkey and top with 2 tablespoons sauce.
   Weeks 9+: Serve 2–4 ounces turkey topped with 2 tablespoons sauce.

▶ **FOR BPD-DS:**
   Weeks 1–3: Puree 2–3 ounces turkey with 2 tablespoons sauce until smooth.
   Weeks 4+: Serve 2–4 ounces turkey with 2 tablespoons sauce.

▶ **FOR OTHERS:**
   Serve 4 ounces turkey with 2 tablespoons sauce.

Calories: 172, **Protein:** 24.91g, **Fat:** 5.29g, **Carbohydrates:** 5.16g, **Cholesterol:** 79.50mg, **Fiber:** 0.90g, **Sodium:** 101.63mg

Sweet-and-Sour Stuffed Cabbage

Is this your Grandma's stuffed cabbage recipe? Kinda-sorta, but not exactly. We omitted the rice and added a citrus tang to the sweet-and-sour sauce.

1 pound lean ground turkey
½ cup low-fat Swiss cheese
½ cup fat-free ricotta cheese
¼ cup egg substitute
½ cup onion, minced
⅛ teaspoon cayenne pepper
⅛ teaspoon pepper
16 large cabbage leaves,
  steamed until soft

Sweet-and-Sour Sauce
  (makes approximately 1 cup):
cooking spray
¼ cup onion, minced
1½ teaspoons fresh ginger,
  minced
1½ teaspoons tomato paste
1 8-ounce can tomato sauce
  (no salt added)
2 tablespoons orange juice
1½ teaspoons red-wine vinegar
1 packet artificial sweetener
  (Splenda or Sweet 'N Low)

1. *To make filling*: In a large bowl, combine ground turkey, cheeses, egg substitute, onion, and seasonings and mix well.
2. *To form cabbage rolls*: Place cabbage leaves on counter top or cutting board. Using a large spoon, place a rounded mound of turkey mixture ¼ inch from edge of each cabbage leaf. Fold top and bottom edges over filling, then starting with filled edge, roll up tightly (you may need to use a toothpick to secure each roll).
3. *To make sauce*: In a large nonstick skillet, heat cooking spray until hot but not smoking. Sauté onions until just soft but not brown, add ginger, and stir for 30 seconds. Add all other sauce ingredients and simmer for 5 minutes.
4. *To cook cabbage rolls*: Place rolls in simmering sauce, cover, and cook over medium-low heat for 20 minutes.

Makes 4 servings (16 rolls)

SERVING GUIDELINES

▶ **FOR LAP-BAND:**
  Weeks 1–4: Puree 1 or 2 cabbage rolls with 2 tablespoons sauce.
  Weeks 5+: Serve 2–4 cabbage rolls with 2 tablespoons sauce.

▶ **FOR BYPASS:**
  Weeks 1–4: Puree 1 or 2 cabbage rolls with 2 tablespoons sauce.
  Weeks 5+: Serve 2–4 cabbage rolls with 2 tablespoons sauce.

▶ **FOR BPD-DS:**
  Weeks 1–3: Puree 1 or 2 cabbage rolls with 2 tablespoons sauce.
  Weeks 4+: Serve 2–4 cabbage rolls with 2 tablespoons sauce.

▶ **FOR OTHERS:**
  Serve 4 cabbage rolls with sauce.

CABBAGE:
Calories: 327.93, **Protein:** 45.89g,
Fat: 5.94g, **Carbohydrates:** 25.54g,
Cholesterol: 73mg, **Fiber:** 5.63g,
Sodium: 264.22mg

SWEET-AND-SOUR SAUCE (2 TABLE-SPOONS):
Calories: 7.70, **Protein:** 0.30g, **Fat:** 0g,
Carbohydrates: 1.74g, **Cholesterol:** 0mg, **Fiber:** 0.29g, **Sodium:** 7.28mg

Asian Turkey-Filled Cabbage Dumplings

MICHELE AND I CHALLENGED OURSELVES TO COME UP WITH A RECIPE FOR DUMPLINGS THAT DOESN'T CONTAIN A LOT OF CARBS, AND THIS DELICIOUS CONCOCTION MADE THE CUT. WE EXPERIMENTED UNTIL WE DISCOVERED THAT CABBAGE COOKED VERY SOFT WORKS THE SAME WAY ASIAN WRAPPER DOUGH DOES.

3 tablespoons egg white
substitute
2 tablespoons light soy sauce
2 tablespoons fresh ginger,
minced
2 garlic cloves, minced
1 teaspoon sesame oil
1 small jalapeño pepper, seeded
and minced
2 packets artificial sweetener
(Splenda or Sweet 'N Low)
1 pound lean ground turkey
breast
⅔ cup minced scallion (white
and green parts)
1 pound (16 large) green cabbage leaves, steamed until
very soft
1 cup water

Dipping Sauce
(makes approximately 1 cup):
¾ cup light soy sauce
¼ cup rice vinegar
2 teaspoons red pepper flakes
or to taste
1 teaspoon sesame oil

1. *To make the dumplings*: In a large bowl, whisk egg white substitute until frothy, then whisk in 2 tablespoons soy sauce, ginger, garlic, sesame oil, jalapeño, and sweetener. Add turkey and scallions and mix until well combined.

2. Place 1 cabbage leaf on a flat surface, either a counter top or a cutting board. Spoon 2 tablespoons of turkey mixture in center of leaf, fold sides of leaf over filling, then fold top and bottom of leaf over sides (you may need to use a toothpick to hold dumpling closed). Repeat until you have filled all cabbage leaves.

3. In a large pot or skillet with a steamer insert or a separate steamer basket, bring water to a boil. Place dumplings into steamer, cover, and steam for 15 minutes.

4. *To make the sauce*: In a small bowl combine sauce ingredients and let stand at room temperature for 10–20 minutes.

MAKES 4 SERVINGS (16 DUMPLINGS)

DUMPLINGS:
   Calories: 190.83, **Protein:** 31.56g, **Fat:** 2.85g, **Carbohydrates:** 10.11g, **Cholesterol:** 55mg, **Fiber:** 4.05g, **Sodium:** 399.21mg

DIPPING SAUCE (2 TABLESPOONS):
   Calories: 14.77, **Protein:** 1.25g, **Fat:** 0.36g, **Carbohydrates:** 1.74g, **Cholesterol:** 0mg, **Fiber:** 0.06g, **Sodium:** 406.57mg

SERVING GUIDELINES

▶ **FOR LAP-BAND:**
   Weeks 1–4: Puree 1–2 dumplings with 2 tablespoons sauce until smooth.
   Weeks 5+: Serve 2–4 dumplings with 2 tablespoons dipping sauce.

▶ **FOR BYPASS:**
   Weeks 1–4: Puree 1–2 dumplings with 2 tablespoons sauce until smooth.
   Weeks 5+: Serve 2–4 dumplings with 2 tablespoons dipping sauce.

▶ **FOR BPD-DS:**
   Weeks 1–3: Puree 1–2 dumplings with 2 tablespoons sauce until smooth.
   Weeks 4+: Serve 2–4 dumplings with 2 tablespoons dipping sauce.

▶ **FOR OTHERS:**
   Serve 4 dumplings with dipping sauce.

Szechuan Turkey and Eggplant

AUTHENTIC? SURE. SPICY? YOU BET. NO ONE WHO TASTES THIS DISH WILL EVER GUESS THAT THIS IS A LOW-FAT, LOW-CALORIE VERSION.

3 tablespoons egg white substitute

¼ cup light soy sauce

2 tablespoons fresh ginger, minced

2 garlic cloves, minced

1 teaspoon sesame oil

1 tablespoon red chili flakes

2 packets artificial sweetener (Splenda or Sweet 'N Low)

1 pound lean ground turkey breast

⅔ cup scallion, minced (white and green parts)

cooking spray

½ cup chopped onion

2 cups cubed fresh eggplant

1 small jalapeño chili, seeded and minced

1 cup cabbage, shredded

¼ cup water

1 tablespoon rice vinegar

1. In a large bowl, whisk egg white until frothy, then whisk in 2 tablespoons soy sauce, ginger, 1 garlic clove, sesame oil, chili flakes, and sweetener. Add turkey and scallion and mix until well combined.

2. Coat a large nonstick skillet with cooking spray and heat until hot but not smoking. Sauté onion and 1 garlic clove about 2 minutes until soft.

3. Stir in eggplant, jalapeño chili, cabbage, water, remaining soy sauce, and rice vinegar, bring to a boil, then cover and reduce heat. Simmer for 10 minutes until eggplant is tender.

4. Add turkey mixture, stirring to combine well. Raise heat to medium and cook for 10 minutes, uncovered, until turkey is cooked through.

MAKES 4 SERVINGS

Calories: 195.95, **Protein:** 31.22, **Fat:** 3.15g, **Carbohydrates:** 10.45g, **Cholesterol:** 55mg, **Fiber:** 2.70g, **Sodium:** 643.97

SERVING GUIDELINES

▶ **FOR LAP-BAND:**
Weeks 1–4: Puree ¼–½ cup turkey-eggplant mixture smooth.
Weeks 5+: Serve ¼–½ cup turkey and eggplant as is.

▶ **FOR BYPASS:**
Weeks 1–4: Puree ¼–½ cup turkey-eggplant mixture smooth.
Weeks 5+: Serve ¼–½ cup turkey and eggplant as is.

▶ **FOR BPD-DS:**
Weeks 1–3: Puree ¼–½ cup turkey-eggplant mixture smooth.
Weeks 4+: Serve ½-1 cup turkey and eggplant as is.

▶ **FOR OTHERS:**
Serve 1 cup turkey and eggplant as is.

Teriyaki Turkey Burgers

SATISFY YOUR CRAVING FOR JAPANESE FLAVOR WITH THIS DELICIOUS WAY TO DRESS UP A BURGER.

1 pound lean ground turkey breast

¼ cup scallions, chopped

1 garlic clove, minced

1 teaspoon fresh ginger, grated

¼ teaspoon black pepper

cooking spray

¼ cup light soy sauce

2 tablespoons rice vinegar

¼ cup dry sherry

1 packet artificial sweetener (Splenda or Sweet 'N Low)

1 cup chopped onion

¼ teaspoon sesame oil

1. In a bowl, combine turkey, scallions, garlic, ginger, and pepper; then divide mixture into 4 equal patties.
2. Coat the bottom of a medium nonstick skillet with cooking spray and heat until hot but not smoking. Cook burgers for 4 minutes on each side until cooked through. Remove burgers from pan and keep warm.
3. Pour soy sauce, rice vinegar, and sherry into pan and stir, scraping up any brown bits. Add sweetener and onion and simmer for 5–7 minutes until onion is soft. Stir in sesame oil.

MAKES 4 SERVINGS

Calories: 174.28, **Protein:** 29.27g, **Fat:** 1.92g, **Carbohydrates:** 6.95g, **Cholesterol:** 55mg, **Fiber:** 0.91g, **Sodium:** 620.39mg

SERVING GUIDELINES

▶ **FOR LAP-BAND:**
Weeks 1–4: Puree ½ cooked burger (2 ounces) with 2 tablespoons sauce.
Weeks 5+: Serve ½–1 cooked burger topped with 2 tablespoons sauce.

▶ **FOR BYPASS:**
Weeks 1–4: Puree ½ cooked burger (2 ounces) with 2 tablespoons sauce.
Weeks 5+: Serve ½–1 cooked burger topped with 2 tablespoons sauce.

▶ **FOR BPD-DS:**
Weeks 1–3: Puree ½ cooked burger (2 ounces) with 2 tablespoons sauce.
Weeks 4+: Serve ½–1 cooked burger topped with 2 tablespoons sauce.

▶ **FOR OTHERS:**
Serve 4 ounces cooked burger topped with 2 tablespoons sauce.

Turkey Loaf with Horseradish Sauce

IT'S HARD TO BELIEVE THAT TURKEY LOAF CAN BE SO LIGHT AND MOIST. WE TOP IT WITH A BOLD, CREAMY HORSERADISH SAUCE. OF COURSE, YOU COULD ALSO TRY IT WITH OUR QUICK TOMATO SAUCE (PAGE 168), GARLIC SAUCE (PAGE 163), OR TIKKA YOGURT SAUCE (PAGE 172). GO AHEAD, EXPERIMENT.

1 pound ground turkey

1 6-ounce can tomato juice

2 tablespoons dried parsley flakes

1 tablespoon dried celery flakes

1 tablespoon dried onion flakes

¼ cup egg substitute, lightly beaten

1 teaspoon pepper

cooking spray

***Horseradish Sauce** (makes approximately 1 cup):*

1 cup fat-free sour cream

3 tablespoons concentrated chicken broth

2 teaspoons sweet paprika

2 tablespoons prepared horse-radish

1. Preheat oven to 350°F.
2. *To make turkey loaf*: In a large bowl, combine turkey, tomato juice, parsley, celery flakes, onion flakes, egg substitute, and pepper and mix well.
3. Coat a baking pan with cooking spray. Mound turkey mixture in center of pan to form a loaf and bake for 1 hour.
4. *To make sauce*: Combine sour cream, concentrated chicken broth, paprika, and horseradish.

MAKES 4 SERVINGS

TURKEY LOAF:
Calories: 151.84, **Protein:** 29.53g, **Fat:** 2.05g, **Carbohydrates:** 4.66g, **Cholesterol:** 55mg, **Fiber:** 0.83g, **Sodium:** 116.52mg

HORSERADISH SAUCE (2 TABLESPOONS):
Calories: 24.09, **Protein:** 1.41g, **Fat:** 0.54g, **Carbohydrates:** 3.79g, **Cholesterol:** 54mg, **Fiber:** 0.05g, **Sodium:** 202mg

SERVING GUIDELINES

▶ **FOR LAP-BAND:**
Weeks 1–4: Puree 2 ounces turkey loaf with 2 tablespoons sauce until smooth.
Weeks 5+: Serve 2–4 ounces turkey loaf with 2 tablespoons sauce.

▶ **FOR BYPASS:**
Weeks 1–4: Puree 2 ounces turkey loaf with 2 tablespoons sauce until smooth.
Weeks 5+: Serve 2–4 ounces turkey loaf with 2 tablespoons sauce.

▶ **FOR BPD-DS:**
Weeks 1–3: Puree 2 ounces turkey loaf with 2 tablespoons sauce until smooth.
Weeks 4+: Serve 2–4 ounces turkey loaf with 2 tablespoons sauce.

▶ **FOR OTHERS:**
Serve 4 ounces turkey loaf with 2 tablespoons sauce.

Sausage and Mushrooms
with Broccoli Rabe

TALK ABOUT PEASANT COOKING—THIS RECIPE IS A COMBINATION OF BOLD, GUTSY FLAVORS. IT'S FOR THE REAL GARLIC LOVER, SO BE PREPARED.

olive oil cooking spray

3 Italian-style lean turkey sausages, hot or sweet

½ pound large white mushrooms, sliced

6 large cloves of garlic, minced (about 3 tablespoons)

4 cups (1 bunch) broccoli rabe, tough ends cut off, coarsely chopped

½ cup chicken broth

½ teaspoon hot pepper flakes

salt and pepper to taste

1. In a medium nonstick skillet, heat cooking spray until hot but not smoking. Sauté sausages for 10 minutes, turning frequently to brown. Remove sausages from pan and cut into thick slices.
2. Pour off any accumulated fat from pan, re-spray, and sauté mushrooms and garlic until slightly browned.
3. Add chopped broccoli rabe, chicken broth, and hot pepper flakes, cover, and steam for 8–10 minutes until soft.
4. In food processor, puree broccoli rabe mixture and sausages until almost smooth (you may need to add additional chicken broth).

MAKES 4 SERVINGS

SERVING GUIDELINES

▶ **FOR LAP-BAND:**
Weeks 1–4: Puree ¼–½ cup until smooth.
Weeks 5+: Serve ¼–½ cup as is.

▶ **FOR BYPASS:**
Weeks 1–4: Puree ¼–½ cup until smooth.
Weeks 5+: Serve ¼–½ cup as is.

▶ **FOR BPD-DS:**
Weeks 1–3: Puree ¼–½ cup until smooth.
Weeks 4+: Serve ½–1 cup as is.

▶ **FOR OTHERS:**
Serve 1 cup as is.

Calories: 160.03, **Protein:** 16.23g, **Fat:** 6.93g, **Carbohydrates:** 12.94g, **Cholesterol:** 41.25mg, **Fiber:** 5.35g, **Sodium:** 375.16mg

No-Noodle Zucchini Lasagna

YES, YOU CAN TAKE OUT THE PASTA AND STILL MAKE GREAT LASAGNA. THIS VERSION IS WHAT'S KNOWN AS "WHITE LASAGNA," WHICH SIMPLY MEANS NO TOMATOES.

½ pound (1 large) zucchini, sliced vertically into 6–8 ⅛-inch slices

½ teaspoon salt

olive oil cooking spray

¾ cup chopped onion

2 garlic cloves, minced

2 cups fresh mushrooms, sliced thin

½ pound lean ground turkey breast

½ cup skim milk

1 10-ounce package frozen chopped spinach, thawed, drained, and squeezed dry

½ cup fat-free ricotta cheese

⅓ cup fresh parsley, chopped

⅛ teaspoon ground nutmeg

¼ teaspoon dried oregano

3 tablespoons grated Parmesan cheese

½ cup part-skim mozzarella cheese, grated

1. Preheat oven to 400°F.
2. Lay zucchini slices on a double thickness of paper towels, sprinkle with salt, cover with more paper towels, and let stand for 15 minutes.
3. Line a cookie sheet with aluminum foil and spray with cooking spray. Lay zucchini slices in 1 layer and bake for 15 minutes. Remove from oven and let cool.
4. Coat bottom of medium skillet with cooking spray and cook over medium heat until hot but not smoking. Brown onion and garlic for 2 minutes; add mushrooms and brown for 2 minutes.
5. Add ground turkey and brown, stirring to break up, for 3 minutes. Remove from heat.
6. In a medium saucepan, bring milk to a boil. Remove from heat and stir in spinach, ricotta cheese, parsley, nutmeg, oregano, and 2 tablespoons of Parmesan cheese.
7. Spoon ½ of spinach mixture in the bottom of an 8-inch square baking pan or casserole dish, then layer on half the mushroom-sausage mixture and lay 3 or 4 slices of zucchini on top. Repeat layers, ending with a zucchini layer. Sprinkle with mozzarella and the remaining 1 tablespoon of Parmesan cheese and bake for 40 minutes.

▷ **HINT:** If you have any leftovers, this freezes well.

MAKES 4 SERVINGS

Calories: 237.49, **Protein:** 29.99g, **Fat:** 7.63g, **Carbohydrates:** 14.30g, **Cholesterol:** 49.11mg, **Fiber:** 4.36g, **Sodium:** 1,341mg

SERVING GUIDELINES

▶ **FOR LAP-BAND:**
Weeks 1–4: Puree ¼–½ cup lasagna till smooth.
Weeks 5+: Serve ¼–½ cup lasagna as is.

▶ **FOR BYPASS:**
Weeks 1–4: Puree ¼–½ cup lasagna till smooth.
Weeks 5+: Serve ¼–½ cup lasagna as is.

▶ **FOR BPD-DS:**
Weeks 1–3: Puree ¼–½ cup lasagna till smooth.
Weeks 4+: Serve ¾–1 cup lasagna as is.

▶ **FOR OTHERS:**
Serve 1 cup lasagna as is.

Un-Pasta Lasagna with Tomato Sauce

THIS IS ANOTHER ONE OF THOSE CLEVER ZUCCHINI LASAGNAS, BUT THIS ONE IS BURSTING
WITH TOMATOES AND TURKEY SAUSAGE, AND LOTS OF REAL SOUTHERN ITALIAN FLAVOR.

*½ pound large zucchini, sliced
vertically ¼ inch thick (about
6–8 slices)*

½ teaspoon salt

olive oil cooking spray

*½ pound low-fat turkey
sausages (sweet or hot
Italian–style), about 2*

1 cup chopped onion

2 garlic cloves, minced

2 tablespoons tomato paste

*1 14.5-ounce can diced toma-
toes, drained*

½ cup dry red wine

*½ packet artificial sweetener
(Splenda or Sweet 'N Low)*

*1 tablespoon fresh basil or 1
teaspoon dried basil, chopped*

*½ cup part-skim mozzarella
cheese, shredded*

½ cup fat-free ricotta cheese

*3 tablespoons grated Parmesan
cheese*

salt and pepper to taste

1. Preheat oven to 400°F.
2. Lay zucchini slices on a double thickness of paper
   towels, sprinkle with salt, cover with more paper
   towels, and let stand for 15 minutes.
3. Line a cookie sheet with aluminum foil and spray
   with cooking spray. Lay zucchini slices in 1 layer and
   bake for 15 minutes, then remove from oven and let
   cool.
4. Coat bottom of a large nonstick skillet with cooking
   spray. Remove sausage meat from casing and sauté
   for 5 minutes over medium heat. Remove from skillet and discard any fat in pan.
5. Re-spray pan and, over medium-high heat, brown
   onion and garlic for 3 minutes.
6. Add tomato paste to onion and cook, stirring, until
   tomato paste begins to darken, about 1 minute.
7. Add diced tomatoes, wine, sweetener, and basil and
   bring to a boil; then reduce heat and simmer for 5
   minutes.
8. In a small bowl, combine mozzarella and ricotta
   cheeses with 2 tablespoons of Parmesan; stir in
   cooked sausage.
9. Spoon ⅓ of tomato sauce in the bottom of an 8-inch
   square baking pan or casserole dish. Lay 3 or 4 slices
   of zucchini on top, then layer on half of the cheese-
   sausage mixture. Repeat layers, ending with sauce
   layer. Sprinkle with remaining 1 tablespoon
   Parmesan cheese and bake for 40 minutes.
10. Serve and add salt and pepper to taste.

MAKES 4 SERVINGS

▷ **HINT:** If you have any leftovers, this freezes well.

Calories: 301.22, **Protein:** 24.58g, **Fat:** 13.06g, **Carbohydrates:** 19.03g, **Cholesterol:** 65mg, **Fiber:** 3.39g, **Sodium:** 1,739.95mg

SERVING GUIDELINES

▶ **FOR LAP-BAND:**
Weeks 1–4: Puree ¼–½ cup lasagna till smooth.
Weeks 5+: Serve ¼–½ cup lasagna as is.

▶ **FOR BYPASS:**
Weeks 1–4: Puree ¼–½ cup lasagna till smooth.
Weeks 5+: Serve ¼–½ cup lasagna as is.

▶ **FOR BPD-DS:**
Weeks 1–3: Puree ¼–½ cup lasagna till smooth.
Weeks 4+: Serve ½–1 cup lasagna as is.

▶ **FOR OTHERS:**
Serve 1 cup lasagna as is.

Sausage and Ricotta Giardiniera

THIS IS A RUSTIC ITALIAN ONE-DISH MEAL THAT INVOLVES A LOT OF CHOPPING AND SUB-STANTIAL COOKING TIME, BUT IT'S EVEN BETTER WHEN COOKED A DAY AHEAD AND REHEATED.

olive oil cooking spray
½ pound Italian-style hot or sweet lean turkey sausages, removed from casings
½ cup onion, coarsely chopped
2 large cloves of garlic, minced
½ pound fresh white mushrooms, cut into eighths
1 cup (1 small) zucchini, cut into coarse cubes
1 cup (1 small) bell pepper, seeded and cut up coarsely
1 14.5-ounce can diced tomatoes
½ cup dry red wine
1 tablespoon fresh basil, minced or 1½ teaspoons dried basil
1 teaspoon hot pepper flakes
½ cup fat-free ricotta cheese
¼ cup part-skim mozzarella cheese, minced or shredded
salt and pepper to taste

1. In a large 4-to-5-quart cooking pot, heat cooking spray until hot but not smoking. Sauté sausage meat for 5 minutes, stirring to break up lumps. Remove from pot with slotted spoon and pour off fat.
2. Add onion, garlic, and mushrooms and cook for about 3 minutes until onion and garlic are just translucent.
3. Stir in sausage, zucchini, bell pepper, tomatoes, wine, and spices, cover pot, and cook over low flame for 1½ hours.
4. Stir in ricotta and mozzarella cheeses; cover and simmer for 5 minutes.

MAKES 8 SERVINGS

SERVING GUIDELINES

▶ **FOR LAP-BAND:**
Weeks 1–4: Puree ½ cup sausage-vegetable-cheese mixture until smooth.
Weeks 5+: Serve ½ cup sausage-vegetable-cheese mixture as is.

▶ **FOR BYPASS:**
Weeks 1–4: Puree ½ cup sausage-vegetable-cheese mixture until smooth.
Weeks 5+: Serve ½ cup sausage-vegetable-cheese mixture as is.

▶ **FOR BPD-DS:**
Weeks 1–3: Puree ½ cup sausage-vegetable-cheese mixture until smooth.
Weeks 4+: Serve ½–1 cup sausage-vegetable-cheese mixture as is.

▶ **FOR OTHERS:**
Serve 1 cup sausage-vegetable-cheese mixture.

Calories: 252.15, **Protein:** 21.20g, **Fat:** 9.40g, **Carbohydrates:** 18.67g, **Cholesterol:** 55.05mg, **Fiber:** 3.95g, **Sodium:** 669.78mg

Braised Pork Tenderloin

THIS IS A SAVORY WAY TO COOK A VERY MILD, LEAN CUT OF MEAT. INSTEAD OF SLICING
THE TENDERLOIN BEFORE COOKING, YOU MARINATE IT TO FLAVOR AND TENDERIZE IT, THEN
QUICKLY BRAISE IT.

1½ cups chopped leeks
1 cup white wine
1 tablespoon Dijon mustard
brown-sugar artificial sweet-
ener (1 teaspoon equivalent)
2 garlic cloves, minced
¼ tablespoon ground thyme
1 tablespoon prepared horse-
radish
salt and pepper to taste
1 pound lean pork tenderloin
cooking spray

1. In a large bowl, combine leeks, ½ cup of wine, mustard, sweetener, garlic, thyme, horseradish, salt, and pepper and pour into a large zip-top plastic bag.
2. Add pork tenderloin to bag, seal it, and shake to coat completely. Chill in refrigerator for 2½ hours.
3. Remove pork from bag, reserving marinade. Coat bottom of large nonstick skillet with cooking spray and heat until hot but not smoking. Sear pork for 2 minutes on each side.
4. Pour remaining ½ cup of wine into reserved marinade in bag, shake well, and pour over pork.
5. Lower heat to medium-low, cover skillet, and braise for 15–20 minutes, until pork is cooked through. Remove pork, slice thin, and keep warm.
6. Simmer sauce for 3 minutes to reduce slightly.

MAKES 4 SERVINGS

SERVING GUIDELINES

▶ **FOR LAP-BAND:**
Weeks 1–4: Puree 2 ounces cooked pork with 2 tablespoons sauce.
Weeks 5–8: Chop 2 ounces cooked pork and top with sauce.
Weeks 9+: Serve 2–4 ounces cooked pork topped with sauce.

▶ **FOR BYPASS:**
Weeks 1–4: Puree 2 ounces cooked pork with 2 tablespoons sauce.
Weeks 5–8: Chop 2 ounces cooked pork and top with sauce.
Weeks 9+: Serve 2–4 ounces cooked pork topped with sauce.

▶ **FOR BPD-DS:**
Weeks 1–3: Puree 2 ounces cooked pork with 2 tablespoons sauce.
Weeks 4+: Serve 3–4 ounces cooked pork topped with sauce.

▶ **FOR OTHERS:**
Serve 4 ounces cooked pork topped with sauce.

Calories: 233.74, **Protein:** 24.31g,
Fat: 7.81g, **Carbohydrates:** 7g,
Cholesterol: 0.08mg, **Fiber:** 0.77g,
Sodium: 125.84mg

Braised Pork with Apples and Onions

THIS RECIPE IS THE EPITOME OF AUTUMN TO ME. IT TAKES THE JUICY SPICINESS OF BAKED APPLES AND COMBINES THEM WITH THE TENDEREST PORK.

1 pound pork tenderloin
olive oil cooking spray
2 cloves of garlic, minced
¼ teaspoon nutmeg
1 tablespoon ground fresh
    grated ginger or 2 teaspoons
    dried ginger
1½ cups onion, cut into ½-
    inch wedges
2 medium Granny Smith
    apples, peeled, cored, and cut
    into ½-inch wedges
2 packets artificial sweetener
    (Splenda or Sweet 'N Low)
½ teaspoon cinnamon
½ cup water

1. Preheat oven to 350°F.
2. Place pork tenderloin in a baking pan that has been coated with cooking spray.
3. In a small bowl, combine garlic, nutmeg, and ginger and rub onto the meat.
4. Surround tenderloin with alternating wedges of onion and apple. Spray onion and apple wedges with cooking spray, sprinkle with sweetener and cinnamon, and pour water over onions and apples.
5. Cover with foil and bake for 20 minutes. Remove foil and bake for 10 minutes more.
6. Slice meat thinly and serve.

MAKES 4 SERVINGS

SERVING GUIDELINES

▶ **FOR LAP-BAND:**
Weeks 1–4: Puree 2 ounces cooked pork with ¼ cup cooked apples and onions.
Weeks 5–8: Chop 2 ounces pork and top with ¼ cup apples and onions.
Weeks 5+: Serve 2–4 ounces pork topped with ¼ cup apples and onions.

▶ **FOR BYPASS:**
Weeks 1–4: Puree 2 ounces cooked pork with ¼ cup cooked apples and onions.
Weeks 5–8: Chop 2 ounces pork and top with ¼ cup apples and onions.
Weeks 5+: Serve 2–4 ounces pork topped with ¼ cup apples and onions.

▶ **FOR BPD-DS:**
Weeks 1–3: Puree 2 ounces cooked pork with ¼ cup cooked apples and onions.
Weeks 4+: Serve 3–4 ounces pork topped with ¼ cup apples and onions.

Calories: 232.47, **Protein:** 23.61g, **Fat:** 7.09g, **Carbohydrates:** 16.94g, **Cholesterol:** 0mg, **Fiber:** 3.04g, **Sodium:** 55.54mg

▶ **FOR OTHERS:**
Serve 4 ounces pork topped with ¼ cup cooked apples and onions.

Indonesian Braised Pork

SORT OF A CROSS BETWEEN ASIAN AND INDIAN, THIS RECIPE IS SURPRISINGLY LIGHT AND LUSCIOUS.

1 pound lean pork tenderloin
cooking spray
½ cup shallots, chopped
½ teaspoon Asian chili paste
  with garlic
1 tablespoon fresh ginger,
  minced
1½ tablespoons light soy sauce
1 cup light unsweetened
  coconut milk
2 tablespoons lime juice

1. Slice tenderloin in ½-inch-thick slices.
2. In a medium nonstick skillet, heat cooking spray over medium-high heat. Brown pork for about 1 minute on each side. Add shallots and sauté until golden.
3. In a small bowl, mix chili paste, ginger, soy sauce, and coconut milk. Add to pan, cover, then lower heat and simmer, turning meat occasionally for about 2 minutes until it is cooked through.
4. Add lime juice, stir, and simmer for 1 more minute.

MAKES 4 SERVINGS

SERVING GUIDELINES

▶ **FOR LAP-BAND:**
  Weeks 1–4: Puree 2 ounces cooked pork with 2 tablespoons sauce until smooth.
  Weeks 5–8: Chop 2 ounces cooked pork and top with sauce.
  Weeks 9+: Serve 2–4 ounces cooked pork with sauce.

▶ **FOR BYPASS:**
  Weeks 1–4: Puree 2 ounces cooked pork with 2 tablespoons sauce until smooth.
  Weeks 5–8: Chop 2 ounces cooked pork and top with sauce.
  Weeks 9+: Serve 2–4 ounces cooked pork with sauce.

▶ **FOR BPD-DS:**
  Weeks 1–3: Puree 2 ounces cooked pork with 2 tablespoons sauce until smooth.
  Weeks 4+: Serve 3–4 ounces cooked pork with sauce.

▶ **FOR OTHERS:**
  Serve 4 ounces cooked pork chop with sauce.

Calories: 333.79, **Protein:** 23.60g,
Fat: 10.70g, **Carbohydrates:** 6.49g,
Cholesterol: 0mg, **Fiber:** 0.15g,
Sodium: 294.97mg

Madeira-Glazed Pork

PORK MEDALLIONS GLAZED WITH A SUBTLY SWEET YET PIQUANT SAUCE REALLY MAKE AN ELEGANT ENTRÉE. THE UNEXPECTED INGREDIENT? VANILLA.

1 pound pork tenderloin
cooking spray
¾ cup shallots, sliced thin
¾ cup Madeira wine
¼ teaspoon vanilla extract
2 tablespoons balsamic vinegar
brown-sugar artificial sweetener
 (1 teaspoon equivalent)
salt and pepper to taste

SERVING GUIDELINES

▶ **FOR LAP-BAND:**
 Weeks 1–4: Puree 2 ounces cooked pork with 2 table-spoons sauce.
 Weeks 5–8: Chop 2 ounces cooked pork and top with sauce.
 Weeks 9+: Serve 2–4 ounces cooked pork and top with sauce.

▶ **FOR BYPASS:**
 Weeks 1–4: Puree 2 ounces cooked pork with 2 table-spoons sauce.
 Weeks 5–8: Chop 2 ounces cooked pork and top with sauce.
 Weeks 9+: Serve 2–4 ounces cooked pork and top with sauce.

▶ **FOR BPD-DS:**
 Weeks 1–4: Puree 2 ounces cooked pork with 2 table-spoons sauce.
 Weeks 5+: Serve 3–4 ounces cooked chop with sauce.

▶ **FOR OTHERS:**
 Serve 4 ounces cooked pork with sauce.

1. Slice tenderloin into ½-inch slices.
2. In a large nonstick skillet, heat cooking spray and sauté pork over medium heat for 4 minutes, turning once. Remove from pan and keep warm.
3. Add shallots to pan and sauté for 3 minutes.
4. Add wine and vanilla to pan, stirring to scrape up any brown bits. Lower heat and simmer 10 minutes until liquid is reduced slightly.
5. Stir in balsamic vinegar and sweetener, return pork and any accumulated juices to pan, and turn once to coat. Add salt and pepper to taste.

MAKES 4 SERVINGS

Calories: 258.64, **Protein:** 23.51g, **Fat:** 6.70g, **Carbohydrates:** 12.28g, **Cholesterol:** 0mg, **Fiber:** 0g, **Sodium:** 175.93mg

Medallions of Pork with Mushrooms

A CREAMY SAUCE WITH THE TANG OF MUSTARD TURNS ORDINARY PORK INTO A DISH THAT TASTES SPECIAL, YET IS EASY ENOUGH FOR EVEN A WORKDAY DINNER.

1 pound pork tenderloin
cooking spray
½ cup shallots, sliced thin
1 cup fresh mushrooms, sliced
  thin
½ cup dry white wine
2 tablespoons concentrated
  chicken broth
¼ teaspoon dried thyme
2 teaspoons whole-grain mus-
  tard
¼ cup fat-free sour cream
salt and pepper to taste

1. Slice tenderloin into ½-inch slices.
2. In a medium nonstick skillet, heat cooking spray until hot but not smoking. Brown pork on both sides, then reduce heat and sauté for 3 minutes, until cooked through. Remove pork from pan.
3. Re-spray pan and sauté shallots and mushrooms, stirring until lightly browned.
4. Stir in wine, scraping up any brown bits. Add concentrated chicken broth and thyme and simmer for 2 minutes.
5. Stir in mustard and sour cream and simmer for 1–2 minutes. Add pork and any accumulated meat juices and turn pork to coat.

MAKES 4 SERVINGS

SERVING GUIDELINES

▶ **FOR LAP-BAND:**
  Weeks 1–4: Puree 2 ounces cooked pork with 2 tablespoons sauce until smooth.
  Weeks 5–8: Chop 2 ounces cooked pork and top with sauce.
  Weeks 9+: Serve 2–4 ounces cooked pork with sauce.

▶ **FOR BYPASS:**
  Weeks 1–4: Puree 2 ounces cooked pork with 2 tablespoons sauce until smooth.
  Weeks 5–8: Chop 2 ounces cooked pork and top with sauce.
  Weeks 9+: Serve 2–4 ounces cooked pork with sauce.

▶ **FOR BPD-DS:**
  Weeks 1–3: Puree 2 ounces cooked pork with 2 tablespoons sauce until smooth.
  Weeks 4+: Serve 3–4 ounces cooked pork with sauce.

▶ **FOR OTHERS:**
  Serve 4 ounces cooked pork topped with sauce.

Calories: 232.33, **Protein:** 25.04g, **Fat:** 7.45g, **Carbohydrates:** 8.28g, **Cholesterol:** 2.50mg, **Fiber:** 0.24g, **Sodium:** 520.77mg

Pork Tenderloin with Fresh Plum Sauce

When we were trying to come up with an Asian-style pork recipe, almost every one we researched contained hoisin sauce (very heavy on sugar). So we concocted this plum sauce, which not only tastes incredible, but is incredibly versatile as well.

1 teaspoon paprika
1 packet artificial sweetener
   (Splenda or Sweet 'N Low)
½ teaspoon allspice
¼ teaspoon nutmeg
½ teaspoon cayenne pepper
1 teaspoon ground ginger
½ teaspoon ground thyme
1 pound lean pork tenderloin
Fresh Plum Sauce (see recipe
   below)

Fresh Plum Sauce
   (makes approximately 1 cup):
cooking spray
½ cup onion, chopped
3 large red or purple plums,
   seeded and chopped
1 clove garlic, minced
1 tablespoon tomato paste
½ small jalapeño pepper,
   seeded and minced
1 tablespoon balsamic vinegar
1 tablespoon light soy sauce
brown-sugar artificial sweetener
   (1 teaspoon equivalent)

1. Preheat oven to 375°F.
2. In a small bowl, mix all spices and sweetener together to form a dry rub.
3. Rub spice mixture all over tenderloin and bake, uncovered, for 15 minutes.
4. Spoon ½ cup of plum sauce (see recipe below) onto tenderloin and bake for another 10 minutes.
5. Slice tenderloin thinly on the diagonal and serve.
6. *To make plum sauce*: Coat a nonstick saucepan with cooking spray. Heat and sauté onion until just translucent. Add all other ingredients and cook over low flame for 10 minutes until thick. Let cool slightly, pour into food processor, and blend until smooth.

Makes 4 servings

▶ **FOR LAP-BAND:**
Weeks 1–4: Puree 2 ounces cooked pork with 2 tablespoons sauce until smooth.
Weeks 5–8: Chop 2 ounces cooked pork and top with 2 tablespoons sauce.
Weeks 9+: Serve 2–4 ounces cooked pork topped with 2 tablespoons sauce.

▶ **FOR BYPASS:**
Weeks 1–4: Puree 2 ounces cooked pork with 2 tablespoons sauce until smooth.
Weeks 5–8: Chop 2 ounces cooked pork and top with 2 tablespoons sauce.
Weeks 9+: Serve 2–4 ounces cooked pork topped with 2 tablespoons sauce.

▶ **FOR BPD-DS:**
Weeks 1–3: Puree 2 ounces cooked pork with 2 tablespoons sauce until smooth.
Weeks 4+: Serve 3–4 ounces cooked pork topped with 2 tablespoons sauce.

▶ **FOR OTHERS:**
Serve 4 ounces cooked pork with 2 tablespoons sauce.

PORK TENDERLOIN:
  Calories: 168, **Protein:** 22.83g, **Fat:** 6.84g, **Carbohydrates:** 1.29g, **Cholesterol:** 0mg, **Fiber:** 0.32g, **Sodium:** 54.15mg

**PLUM SAUCE
(2 TABLESPOONS):**
  Calories: 12.11, **Protein:** 0.34g, **Fat:** 0.09g, **Carbohydrates:** 2.70g, **Cholesterol:** 0mg, **Fiber:** .32g, **Sodium:** 49.06mg

Pork with Onions and Capers

CAPERS, THOSE TENDER LITTLE BUDS THAT PACK A LOT OF FLAVOR, ADD AN UNEXPECTED HINT OF SHARPNESS TO A LOVELY CREAMY ONION SAUCE.

1 pound pork tenderloin
cooking spray
1½ cup onion, sliced thin
½ cup dry vermouth
¼ cup water
2 teaspoons concentrated
* chicken broth*
2 tablespoons capers, rinsed
* and drained*
¼ cup fat-free sour cream
salt and pepper to taste

1. Slice tenderloin into ½-inch slices.
2. In a large nonstick skillet, heat cooking spray until hot but not smoking. Sauté the pork for about 2 minutes on each side, then remove from pan.
3. Re-spray pan and add onion. Cook, stirring, for about 3–4 minutes, until onion just starts to brown.
4. Add vermouth and water and simmer for 3–4 minutes, until liquid is reduced to about ¼ cup.
5. Stir in concentrated chicken broth and capers; raise heat to high and bring onion mixture to boil, then cook until reduced by half.
6. Turn off heat, stir in sour cream, and add sliced pork and any accumulated meat juices. Turn pork slices to coat, and serve. Salt and pepper to taste.

MAKES 4 SERVINGS

SERVING GUIDELINES

▶ **FOR LAP-BAND:**
Weeks 1–4: Puree 2 ounces cooked pork with 2 tablespoons onion sauce.
Weeks 5–8: Chop 2 ounces cooked pork and top with onion sauce.
Weeks 9+: Serve 2–4 ounces cooked pork topped with onion sauce.

▶ **FOR BYPASS:**
Weeks 1–4: Puree 2 ounces cooked pork with 2 tablespoons onion sauce.
Weeks 5–8: Chop 2 ounces cooked pork and top with onion sauce.
Weeks 9+: Serve 2–4 ounces cooked pork topped with onion sauce.

▶ **FOR BPD-DS:**
Weeks 1–3: Puree 2 ounces cooked pork with 2 tablespoons onion sauce.
Weeks 4+: Serve 3–4 ounces cooked pork topped with onion sauce.

▶ **FOR OTHERS:**
Serve 4 ounces cooked pork topped with onion sauce.

Calories: 225.64, **Protein:** 24.17g, **Fat:** 6.86g, **Carbohydrates:** 7.37g, **Cholesterol:** 2.50mg, **Fiber:** 0.78g, **Sodium:** 374.63mg

Thai Caramel Pork

LIKE THE BEST THAI RECIPES, THIS ONE HAS ALL THE TASTES—SALTY, SWEET, SOUR, AND HOT. IT MIGHT SOUND CONTRADICTORY, BUT TRUST ME; THE WAY THESE TASTES ARE COMBINED IN THIS SAUCE, THEY COMPLEMENT ONE ANOTHER PERFECTLY.

*1 cup unsweetened light
    coconut milk*
*brown-sugar artificial sweetener
    (1 teaspoon equivalent)*
¼ cup Asian fish sauce
½ cup shallots, sliced thin
½ teaspoon cayenne pepper
cooking spray
1 pound pork tenderloin
1 tablespoon rice vinegar

1. Pour coconut milk and brown-sugar sweetener into a heavy saucepan and simmer, uncovered, over medium-high heat until slightly thickened and light brown.
2. Add fish sauce and shallots, reduce heat, and cook, stirring occasionally, for about 5 minutes. Add cayenne pepper and set aside to cool.
3. In a large nonstick skillet, heat cooking spray until hot but not smoking. Sear pork on 1 side for about 2 minutes, then turn and sear on the other side for 1 minute.
4. Reduce heat to medium, cover skillet, and cook pork for 10–12 minutes, until cooked through. Remove pork from pan and slice thinly on the diagonal.
5. De-glaze pan with vinegar, scraping up any brown bits. Add reserved sauce and stir over low heat for 2 minutes. Add pork to coat and turn off heat.

MAKES 4 SERVINGS

SERVING GUIDELINES

▶ **FOR LAP-BAND:**
Weeks 1–4: Puree 2 ounces cooked pork with 2 tablespoons sauce.
Weeks 5–8: Chop 2 ounces cooked pork and top with sauce.
Weeks 9+: Serve 2–4 ounces cooked pork topped with sauce.

▶ **FOR BYPASS:**
Weeks 1–4: Puree 2 ounces cooked pork with 2 tablespoons sauce.
Weeks 5–8: Chop 2 ounces cooked pork and top with sauce.
Weeks 9+: Serve 2–4 ounces cooked pork topped with sauce.

▶ **FOR BPD-DS:**
Weeks 1–3: Puree 2 ounces cooked pork with 2 tablespoons sauce.
Weeks 3+: Serve 3–4 ounces cooked pork topped with sauce.

▶ **FOR OTHERS:**
Serve 4 ounces cooked pork topped with sauce.

Calories: 228.49, **Protein:** 23.92g,
Fat: 10.73g, **Carbohydrates:** 6.01g,
Cholesterol: 0mg, **Fiber:** 0.06g,
Sodium: 1,165.17mg

Cider-Glazed Pork Chops

HERE IS ANOTHER ONE OF THOSE PERFECT PAIRINGS—PORK AND APPLE CIDER. THIS SIM-
PLE RECIPE EMPHASIZES THE TANG OF THE FRUIT, WITHOUT BEING TOO SWEET.

cooking spray
1 pound lean boneless pork
*   chops*
1 cup apple cider
brown-sugar artificial sweetener
*   (1 teaspoon equivalent)*
1 teaspoon Dijon mustard
½ cup fat-free, low-sodium
*   chicken broth*
2 tablespoons cider vinegar

1. In a medium nonstick skillet, heat cooking spray until hot but not smoking. Sauté pork chops for 2 minutes on each side, then remove chops and keep warm.
2. Stir together cider and brown-sugar substitute and add to skillet. Simmer, uncovered, for 1 minute; then add mustard, broth, and vinegar, stirring to scrape up any brown bits. Simmer for 5 minutes until sauce is slightly thickened.
3. Return chops to pan with any meat juices that have accumulated and turn chops in sauce to coat. Simmer for 2 more minutes, then serve.

MAKES 4 SERVINGS

SERVING GUIDELINES

▶ **FOR LAP-BAND:**
   Weeks 1–4: Puree 2 ounces cooked pork with 2 tablespoons sauce until smooth.
   Weeks 5–8: Chop 2 ounces cooked pork and top with sauce.
   Weeks 9+: Serve 2–4 ounces cooked pork with sauce.

▶ **FOR BYPASS:**
   Weeks 1–4: Puree 2 ounces cooked pork with 2 tablespoons sauce until smooth.
   Weeks 5–8: Chop 2 ounces cooked pork and top with sauce.
   Weeks 9+: Serve 2–4 ounces cooked pork with sauce.

▶ **FOR BPD-DS:**
   Weeks 1–3: Puree 2 ounces cooked pork with 2 tablespoons sauce until smooth.
   Weeks 4+: Serve 3–4 ounces cooked pork with sauce.

▶ **FOR OTHERS:**
   Serve 4 ounces cooked pork chop with sauce.

Calories: 257.40, **Protein:** 26.04g, **Fat:** 13.55g, **Carbohydrates:** 8.20g, **Cholesterol:** 0.03mg, **Fiber:** 0.02g, **Sodium:** 82.42mg

Smoked Pork Chops with Pineapple

THIS IS A SLIGHTLY MORE SOPHISTICATED VERSION OF THE CLASSIC HAM STEAK WITH PINEAPPLE SLICES—AND, YES, WE PURPOSELY LEFT OUT THE MARASCHINO CHERRY.

cooking spray

1 pound lean, precooked smoked boneless pork chops or ham steaks

½ cup onion, chopped

1 tablespoon balsamic vinegar

2 teaspoons concentrated chicken broth

½ cup water

brown-sugar artificial sweetener (1 teaspoon equivalent)

½ cup fresh pineapple, diced

½ teaspoon chili powder

1. In a large nonstick skillet, heat cooking spray until hot but not smoking. Sauté pork for 2 minutes on 1 side, turn, and cook for 2 minutes on the other. Remove from pan and keep warm.

2. Add onions to the pan and sauté for 2 minutes, until soft.

3. Add balsamic vinegar, concentrated chicken broth, water, and brown sugar sweetener, and stir to scrape up any brown bits. Stir in pineapple and chili powder, lower heat, and simmer for 3 minutes.

MAKES 4 SERVINGS

Calories: 164.55, **Protein:** 22.53g, **Fat:** 5.11g, **Carbohydrates:** 5.55g, **Cholesterol:** 51.03mg, **Fiber:** 0.70g, **Sodium:** 1,650.50mg

SERVING GUIDELINES

▶ **FOR LAP-BAND:**
Weeks 1–4: Puree 2 ounces cooked pork chop with 2 table-spoons sauce.
Weeks 5–8: Chop 2 ounces cooked pork chop and top with sauce.
Weeks 9+: Serve 2–4 ounces cooked pork chop topped with sauce.

▶ **FOR BYPASS:**
Weeks 1–4: Puree 2 ounces cooked pork chop with 2 table-spoons sauce.
Weeks 5–8: Chop 2 ounces cooked pork chop and top with sauce.
Weeks 9+: Serve 2–4 ounces cooked pork chop topped with sauce.

▶ **FOR BPD-DS:**
Weeks 1–4: Puree 2 ounces cooked pork chop with 2 table-spoons sauce.
Weeks 5+: Serve 2–4 ounces cooked pork chop topped with sauce.

▶ **FOR OTHERS:**
Serve 4 ounces cooked pork chop topped with sauce.

Beef Bordelaise

THIS DISH IS SO GOOD THAT I OFTEN DOUBLE IT AND FREEZE HALF OR SERVE IT TWO DAYS IN A ROW. THE SECRET INGREDIENT? THE ORANGE PEEL. IT REALLY ADDS A BIT OF ZING.

olive oil cooking spray

1 pound lean beef round, trimmed and cut into 1-inch cubes

1½ cups onion, chopped

2 large garlic cloves, chopped

½ cup dry red wine

½ cup fat-free, low-sodium beef broth

1 cup tomato, chopped

1 6-ounce can tomato juice

1 3 x 1-inch piece of orange peel

1 teaspoon Worcestershire sauce

1 teaspoon chopped fresh rosemary or ½ teaspoon dried rosemary

½ pound peeled baby carrots

▷ **HINT:** This recipe can be made 3 days ahead and refrigerated.

1. In a heavy stewpot, heat cooking spray until hot but not smoking. Brown beef on all sides and remove to a bowl.
2. Discard any fat accumulated in pot. Add onion and garlic to pot and cook over medium heat, stirring, for 2 minutes, until golden.
3. Add wine, broth, tomato, tomato juice, orange peel, Worcestershire, and rosemary and bring to a boil. Add beef and any meat juices that have accumulated.
4. Cover and lower heat; simmer for 30 minutes.
5. Stir in carrots, cover, and simmer for 1½ hours.
6. Uncover, raise heat to medium-high, and cook for 15 minutes, until liquid in pot reduces and is slightly thickened.

MAKES 4 SERVINGS

SERVING GUIDELINES

▶ **FOR LAP-BAND:**
Weeks 1–4: Puree 2 ounces cooked beef with 2 tablespoons vegetables and sauce.
Weeks 5–8: Chop 2 ounces cooked beef and top with vegetables and sauce.
Weeks 9+: Serve 2–4 ounces cooked beef topped with vegetables and sauce.

▶ **FOR BYPASS:**
Weeks 1–4: Puree 2 ounces cooked beef with 2 tablespoons vegetables and sauce.
Weeks 5–8: Chop 2 ounces cooked beef and top with vegetables and sauce.
Weeks 9+: Serve 2–4 ounces cooked beef topped with vegetables and sauce.

▶ **FOR BPD-DS:**
Weeks 1–3: Puree 2–3 ounces cooked beef with 2 tablespoons vegetables and sauce.
Weeks 4+: Serve 3–4 ounces cooked beef topped with vegetables and sauce.

▶ **FOR OTHERS:**
Serve 4 ounces cooked beef topped with vegetables and sauce.

Calories: 243.93, **Protein:** 26.64g, **Fat:** 4.40g, **Carbohydrates:** 15.83g, **Cholesterol:** 60.08mg, **Fiber:** 3.14g, **Sodium:** 133.26mg

Mom's Pot Roast

Yes, this really is my mother's pot roast recipe. The coffee, while not an expected ingredient, makes this pot roast intensely flavorful.

cooking spray

2 pounds lean beef brisket

1½ cups onion, cut in chunks

2 garlic cloves, minced

2 tablespoons sweet paprika

1 14.5-ounce can beef broth

1 cup strong brewed coffee

1 cup water

2 tablespoons concentrated
    beef broth

2 bay leaves

1 ounce dried mushrooms

1½ cups carrot, cut in chunks

¾ pound green beans, ends
    trimmed

salt and pepper to taste

▷ **HINT:** This dish can be made a day ahead and refrigerated until you're ready to serve. Just remember to skim off the fat before reheating.

Calories: 231.11, **Protein:** 26.72g,
Fat: 8.65g, **Carbohydrates:** 10.72g,
Cholesterol: 70.31mg, **Fiber:** 2.71g,
Sodium: 681.34mg

1. In a 4-to-5-quart nonstick Dutch oven, heat cooking spray until hot but not smoking. Place meat in oven and brown on both sides, about 5 minutes. Remove meat from pot and pour off accumulated fat.

2. Place onion, garlic, and paprika in pot, stir, cover, and cook over medium heat for 5–7 minutes, or until onion is softened.

3. Add meat on top of onion mixture and pour in beef broth, coffee, and water. Stir in concentrated beef broth, cover pot, and bring to a boil. Then add bay leaves, mushrooms, and carrot, lower heat to simmer, cover, and cook for 1½ hours.

4. Remove meat from pot and slice thinly on diagonal.

5. Add meat back to pot, place green beans on top, cover, and cook for another ½ hour.

Makes 8 servings

SERVING GUIDELINES

▶ **FOR LAP-BAND:**
Weeks 1–4: Puree 2 ounces cooked beef with 2 tablespoons vegetables and sauce.
Weeks 5–8: Chop 2 ounces cooked beef with vegetables and sauce.
Weeks 9+: Serve 2–4 ounces cooked beef with vegetables and sauce.

▶ **FOR BYPASS:**
Weeks 1–4: Puree 2 ounces cooked beef with 2 tablespoons vegetables and sauce.
Weeks 5–8: Chop 2 ounces cooked beef with vegetables and sauce.
Weeks 9+: Serve 2–4 ounces cooked beef with vegetables and sauce.

▶ **FOR BPD-DS:**
Weeks 1–3: Puree 2 ounces cooked beef with 2 tablespoons vegetables and sauce.
Weeks 4+: Serve 2–4 ounces cooked beef with vegetables and sauce.

▶ **FOR OTHERS:**
Serve 4 ounces of cooked beef with vegetables and sauce.

Beef Stroganoff

EVERYTHING ABOUT THIS RECIPE IS AUTHENTIC TO THE ORIGINAL RUSSIAN DISH, EXCEPT WE LEFT OUT ALL THE FAT.

cooking spray

2 cloves garlic, minced

1 pound lean eye round, cut into 1-inch cubes

1 6-ounce can tomato sauce

½ cup dry red wine

1 cup fresh mushrooms, sliced

1 bay leaf

½ cup fat-free sour cream

salt and pepper to taste

1. Coat bottom of large nonstick skillet with cooking spray and sauté garlic for 1 minute, until soft. Add meat and brown, stirring, for 3 minutes.
2. Add tomato sauce, wine, mushrooms, and bay leaf and simmer, covered, over low heat for about 1½ hours.
3. Turn off heat and stir in sour cream. Add salt and pepper to taste.

MAKES 4 SERVINGS

SERVING GUIDELINES

▶ **FOR LAP-BAND:**
Weeks 1–4: Puree 2 ounces cooked meat with 2 tablespoons sauce.
Weeks 5–8: Chop 2 ounces cooked meat and top with sauce.
Weeks 9+: Serve 2–4 ounces meat with sauce.

▶ **FOR BYPASS:**
Weeks 1–4: Puree 2 ounces cooked meat with 2 tablespoons sauce.
Weeks 5–8: Chop 2 ounces cooked meat and top with sauce.
Weeks 9+: Serve 2–4 ounces meat with sauce.

▶ **FOR BPD-DS:**
Weeks 1–3: Puree 2 ounces cooked meat with 2 tablespoons sauce
Weeks 4+: Serve 3–4 ounces meat with sauce.

▶ **FOR OTHERS:**
Serve 4 ounces meat with sauce.

Calories: 228.52, **Protein:** 27.20g, **Fat:** 3.64g, **Carbohydrates:** 10.42g, **Cholesterol:** 65.08mg, **Fiber:** 0.98g, **Sodium:** 254.17mg

Flank Steak Basquaise

RECIPES FROM THE BASQUE SECTION OF SPAIN OFTEN USE A SAVORY MIXTURE OF BELL PEPPER, ONION, AND TOMATO. WE ADDED WINE AND MUSHROOMS JUST 'CAUSE WE LIKE THEM.

1 pound lean flank steak
olive oil cooking spray
½ cup chopped onion
2 cloves garlic, chopped
½ cup red bell pepper, seeded and chopped
½ pound fresh mushrooms, sliced
½ cup dry red wine
½ cup chopped plum tomatoes
2 teaspoons concentrated beef broth
salt and pepper to taste

1. Place flank steak on broiling pan and score top so it won't curl. Broil for 3–5 minutes on each side until medium rare.
2. While steak is broiling, heat cooking spray in a medium nonstick skillet until it's hot but not smoking. Sauté onions and garlic for 3 minutes until lightly browned.
3. Add pepper and mushrooms and cook, covered, for 3–5 minutes until soft. Add wine, tomatoes, and beef broth concentrate and cook, stirring occasionally, until liquid is reduced by half.
4. Slice steak, on diagonal, very thin. Add salt and pepper to taste.

MAKES 4 SERVINGS

SERVING GUIDELINES

▶ **FOR LAP-BAND:**
  Weeks 1–4: Puree 2 ounces cooked steak with 2 tablespoons sauce.
  Weeks 5–8: Chop 2 ounces cooked steak and top with sauce.
  Weeks 9+: Serve 2–4 ounces of steak with sauce.

▶ **FOR BYPASS:**
  Weeks 1–4: Puree 2 ounces cooked steak with 2 tablespoons of sauce.
  Weeks 5–8: Chop 2 ounces cooked steak and top with sauce.
  Weeks 9+: Serve 2–4 ounces steak with sauce.

▶ **FOR BPD-DS:**
  Weeks 1–3: Puree 2 ounces cooked steak with 2 tablespoons sauce.
  Weeks 4+: Serve 3–4 ounces steak with sauce.

▶ **FOR OTHERS:**
  Serve 4 ounces steak with sauce.

Calories: 229.94, **Protein:** 24.18g, **Fat:** 9.45g, **Carbohydrates:** 9.12g, **Cholesterol:** 65mg, **Fiber:** 2.03g, **Sodium:** 292.07mg

London Broil with Horseradish Cream

THE BRITISH TRADITIONALLY SERVE BEEF WITH HORSERADISH. HERE IS A FLAVORFUL VARIATION ON THAT CLASSIC THEME.

1 pound lean London broil (top round or flank steak)

1½ teaspoons garlic powder

1 tablespoon lemon-pepper

½ cup fat-free sour cream

1 tablespoon concentrated beef broth

2 tablespoons prepared horse-radish

SERVING GUIDELINES

▶ **FOR LAP-BAND:**
Weeks 1–4: Puree 2 ounces cooked beef with 2 table-spoons sauce.
Weeks 5–8: Chop 2 ounces cooked beef and top with sauce.
Weeks 9+: Serve 2–4 ounces cooked beef topped with sauce.

▶ **FOR BYPASS:**
Weeks 1–4: Puree 2 ounces cooked beef with 2 table-spoons sauce.
Weeks 5–8: Chop 2 ounces cooked beef and top with sauce.
Weeks 9+: Serve 2–4 ounces cooked beef topped with sauce.

▶ **FOR BPD-DS:**
Weeks 1–3: Puree 2–3 ounces cooked beef with 2 table-spoons sauce.
Weeks 4+: Serve 3–4 ounces cooked beef topped with sauce.

▶ **FOR OTHERS:**
Serve 4 ounces steak with sauce.

1. Sprinkle London broil with garlic powder and lemon-pepper.
2. Place in nonstick broiling pan and broil for 4 minutes on each side for medium rare.
3. While steak is broiling, combine sour cream, concentrated beef broth. and horseradish in a small bowl.
4. Slice steak thinly on diagonal, pour sauce over it, and serve.

MAKES 4 SERVINGS

Calories: 182, **Protein:** 28.14g, **Fat:** 5.06g, **Carbohydrates:** 8.29g, **Cholesterol:** 65.08mg, **Fiber:** 0.04g, **Sodium:** 722.91mg

Soy-Mustard Glazed Beef

ALL THE INGREDIENTS IN THIS DISH SHOULDN'T WORK TOGETHER, BUT THEY DO. THE GLAZE CREATES A SEARED CRUST ON THE MEAT, WHILE THE CREAMY SAUCE COMPLIMENTS IT PERFECTLY.

⅓ cup light soy sauce

2 tablespoons Dijon mustard

1 tablespoon lemon juice

4 cloves garlic, quartered

1½ teaspoons fresh ginger, minced

½ teaspoon dried thyme

½ teaspoon fresh ground black pepper

½ teaspoon fresh rosemary

1 pound lean top round or flank steak

½ cup fat-free sour cream

1 tablespoon concentrated beef broth

¼ teaspoon sesame oil

1. *To make glaze*: in a mini-processor or blender, combine soy sauce, mustard, lemon juice, garlic, ginger, thyme, pepper, and rosemary and process until smooth. Reserve 2 tablespoons to make sauce.
2. Brush top of steak with glaze mixture and broil 3–4 minutes. Turn steak, brush other side with glaze, and broil 3–4 minutes longer for medium rare.
3. In a small bowl, combine reserved glaze with sour cream, concentrated beef broth, and sesame oil.
4. Slice steak thinly on the diagonal, pour sauce over it, and serve.

MAKES 4 SERVINGS

SERVING GUIDELINES

► **FOR LAP-BAND:**
Weeks 1–4: Puree 2 ounces cooked beef with 2 tablespoons sauce.
Weeks 5–8: Chop 2 ounces cooked beef and top with sauce.
Weeks 9+: Serve 2–4 ounces cooked beef with sauce.

► **FOR BYPASS:**
Weeks 1–4: Puree 2 ounces cooked beef with 2 tablespoons sauce.
Weeks 5–8: Chop 2 ounces cooked beef and top with sauce.
Weeks 9+: Serve 2–4 ounces cooked beef with sauce.

► **FOR BPD-DS:**
Weeks 1–3: Puree 2 ounces cooked beef with 2 tablespoons sauce.
Weeks 3+: Serve 3–4 ounces cooked beef with sauce.

► **FOR OTHERS:**
Serve 4 ounces steak with sauce.

Calories: 248.70, **Protein:** 26.64g, **Fat:** 9.97g, **Carbohydrates:** 11.68g, **Cholesterol:** 70.15mg, **Fiber:** 0.30g, **Sodium:** 1,188.01mg

Savory Onion and Mushroom Burgers

YOU WON'T MISS THE HAMBURGER BUNS WHEN YOU TASTE HOW DELECTABLE THESE BURGERS ARE.

cooking spray
1 large sweet onion, sliced thin
and separated into rings
(about 1½ cups)
2 cups fresh mushrooms, sliced
1 tablespoon sweet paprika
¼ teaspoon ground red pepper
½ teaspoon dried thyme
¼ teaspoon black pepper,
freshly ground
1 pound lean ground round
2 tablespoons balsamic vinegar
2 tablespoons concentrated
beef broth
½ cup water
2 tablespoons prepared horse-
radish

1. Coat bottom of a medium non-stick skillet with cooking spray. Sauté onion rings over medium-high heat for 5 minutes until slightly browned.
2. Add mushrooms and cover, reduce heat to medium, and cook for 5 minutes until mushrooms give up their liquid. Remove onion-mushroom mixture from pan and reserve the liquid.
3. While onions and mushrooms are cooking, mix paprika, red pepper, thyme, and black pepper in a shallow bowl.
4. Divide meat into 4 burgers; dredge burgers on both sides in spices.
5. Re-coat pan with cooking spray and sauté burgers over medium-high heat on 1 side for 4 minutes. Flip burgers over, cover pan, and cook for 3–4 more minutes until medium-rare. Remove burgers from pan and discard any accumulated fat.
6. De-glaze the pan with the balsamic vinegar, scraping up any brown bits. Add concentrated broth, water, and horseradish, bring to a simmer, and add reserved onion-mushroom mixture.
7. Simmer, uncovered, stirring occasionally for 3 minutes until slightly reduced.

Makes 4 servings

Calories: 202.87, **Protein:** 26.21g, **Fat:** 6.89g, **Carbohydrates:** 11.44g, **Cholesterol:** 62mg, **Fiber:** 1.89g, **Sodium:** 957.60mg

SERVING GUIDELINES

▶ **FOR LAP-BAND:**
Weeks 1–4: Puree ½ cooked burger (2 ounces) with 2 tablespoons onion-mushroom sauce.
Weeks 5+: Serve ½–1 cooked burger topped with onion-mushroom sauce.

▶ **FOR BYPASS:**
Weeks 1–4: Puree ½ cooked burger (2 ounces) with 2 tablespoons onion-mushroom sauce.
Weeks 5+: Serve ½–1 cooked burger topped with onion-mushroom sauce.

▶ **FOR BPD-DS:**
Weeks 1–3: Puree ½ cooked burger (2 ounces) with 2 tablespoons onion-mushroom sauce.
Weeks 4+: Serve ½–1 cooked burger topped with onion-mushroom sauce.

▶ **FOR OTHERS:**
Serve 1 cooked burger topped with onion-mushroom sauce.

Tuscan Veal Stew

This is a light, brightly spiced stew that can be made a day or two ahead and kept in the refrigerator. I usually save this recipe for "Sunday cooking."

1 14.5-ounce can fat-free, low-sodium chicken broth
1 cup (8) sun-dried tomatoes (not oil-packed), quartered
olive oil cooking spray
1 pound lean veal, cut into 1-inch cubes
½ cup white wine
1 cup fresh mushrooms, sliced
½ cup plain, fat-free yogurt
1 small fresh red or green Serrano or jalapeño pepper, seeded and sliced in half
1 teaspoon fresh rosemary
salt and pepper to taste

1. In shallow glass bowl, heat chicken broth in microwave on HIGH for 45 seconds. Soak sun-dried tomatoes in broth for 15 minutes.
2. Coat bottom of 4-to-5-quart nonstick cooking pot with cooking spray and heat over medium-high flame until hot but not smoking. Brown veal for 3 minutes, turning, until golden (if necessary, brown in 2 batches). Remove to bowl.
3. De-glaze pot with wine, scraping up any brown bits. Add veal and any meat juices that have accumulated. Add sun-dried tomatoes and broth, mushrooms, yogurt, hot pepper, and rosemary.
4. Reduce heat to low and simmer, covered, stirring occasionally, about 1¼ hours, until veal is tender.
5. Discard chili pepper and add salt and pepper to taste.

MAKES 4 SERVINGS

SERVING GUIDELINES

▶ **FOR LAP-BAND:**
Weeks 1–4: Puree 2 ounces cooked veal with 2 tablespoons vegetables and sauce.
Weeks 5–8: Chop 2 ounces cooked veal and top with vegetables and sauce.
Weeks 9+: Serve 2–4 ounces cooked veal topped with vegetables and sauce.

▶ **FOR BYPASS:**
Weeks 1–4: Puree 2 ounces cooked veal with 2 tablespoons vegetables and sauce.
Weeks 5–8: Chop 2 ounces cooked veal and top with vegetables and sauce.
Weeks 9+: Serve 2–4 ounces cooked veal topped with vegetables and sauce.

▶ **FOR BPD-DS:**
Weeks 1–3: Puree 2 ounces cooked veal with 2 tablespoons vegetables and sauce.
Weeks 4+: Serve 3–4 ounces cooked veal topped with vegetables and sauce.

▶ **FOR OTHERS:**
Serve 4 ounces cooked veal topped with vegetables and sauce.

Calories: 189.15, **Protein:** 26.54g, **Fat:** 3.45g, **Carbohydrates:** 7.48g, **Cholesterol:** 94.96mg, **Fiber:** 0.79g, **Sodium:** 525.36mg

Greek Lamb Burgers with Yogurt-Mint Sauce

INSTEAD OF CLASSIC GRILLED LAMB, WE'VE TAKEN A CLASSIC RECIPE AND TURNED IT INTO BURGERS SO YOU CAN ENJOY THIS DISH EVEN ON A WEEKNIGHT.

¾ cup scallions, about 3 or 4, white and light green parts only

1 pound lean ground lamb

1 teaspoon cumin

1 teaspoon coriander

salt and pepper to taste

olive oil cooking spray

Yogurt-Mint Sauce *(makes approximately 1 cup):*

½ teaspoon lemon zest

½ cup mint leaves

1 small garlic clove, quartered

¾ cup plain, fat-free yogurt

1 teaspoon cumin

1 tablespoon fresh lemon juice

2 teaspoons concentrated chicken broth

1. In a mini-processor or chopper, chop scallions.
2. Mix scallions, lamb, and seasonings in bowl so they are well blended. Form into 4 burgers.
3. In a medium nonstick skillet, heat cooking spray until hot but not smoking. Place burgers in skillet, turn heat to medium, and cover. Cook meat on 1 side for 3 minutes, then turn over and cook, covered, for 3 minutes more.
4. While meat is cooking, mix lemon zest, mint, and garlic in mini-processor or chopper and chop.
5. In a medium-size bowl, mix yogurt, cumin, lemon juice, and concentrated chicken broth. Add ground mint mixture and mix well.
6. Remove burgers from the skillet and drain on paper towel. Pour sauce over the burgers and serve.

MAKES 4 SERVINGS

SERVING GUIDELINES

▶ **FOR LAP-BAND:**
Weeks 1–4: Puree ½ cooked burger (2 ounces) with 2 tablespoons sauce until smooth.
Weeks 5+: Serve ½–1 cooked burger (2–4 ounces) topped with 2 tablespoons sauce.

▶ **FOR BYPASS:**
Weeks 1–4: Puree ½ cooked burger (2 ounces) with 2 tablespoons sauce until smooth.
Weeks 5+: Serve ½–1 cooked burger (2–4 ounces) topped with 2 tablespoons sauce.

▶ **FOR BPD-DS:**
Weeks 1–4: Puree ½ cooked burger (2 ounces) with 2 tablespoons sauce until smooth.
Weeks 5+: Serve ½–1 cooked burger (2–4 ounces) topped with 2 tablespoons sauce.

▶ **FOR OTHERS:**
Serve 1 cooked burger topped with sauce.

BURGERS:
Calories: 331.39, **Protein:** 19.32g, **Fat:** 26.78g, **Carbohydrates:** 1.98g, **Cholesterol:** 82.78mg, **Fiber:** 1.09g, **Sodium:** 71.31mg

YOGURT-MINT SAUCE (2 TABLESPOONS):
Calories: 15.25, **Protein:** 1.08g, **Fat:** 0.13g, **Carbohydrates:** 2.52g, **Cholesterol:** 0.31mg, **Fiber:** 0.63g, **Sodium:** 51.92mg

Moussaka

Here is a lighter version of this classic Greek dish. We substituted ground turkey for half of the ground lamb and used skim milk for the custard, but it still tastes authentic. It is kind of labor intensive, so why not make it for Sunday dinner?

1 large eggplant, about 1½
  pounds
½ teaspoon salt
cooking spray
½ pound lean ground lamb
½ pound lean ground turkey
1 cup onion, finely chopped
1 clove garlic, minced
¼ pound (about 4–5 large)
  mushrooms, coarsely
  chopped
¼ cup red wine
1 8-ounce can tomato sauce
1 tablespoon dried parsley
  flakes
1 tablespoon chopped fresh
  oregano or 1½ teaspoons
  dried oregano
¼ teaspoon cinnamon
salt and pepper to taste

Custard Topping:
1½ cups skim milk
½ cup egg substitute
½ cup grated Parmesan cheese
  plus 2 tablespoons grated
  Parmesan cheese

1. Preheat oven to 400°F.
2. Cut the ends off the eggplant and slice horizontally into ¼-inch-thick slices. Line a colander with eggplant slices, sprinkle with salt, and let drain for 30 minutes.
3. Coat a large nonstick skillet with cooking spray and cook lamb and turkey over medium heat, stirring vigorously to separate. Brown for about 5 minutes, then drain off fat.
4. Add onions, garlic, and mushrooms and cook over medium heat about 3 minutes. Add wine, tomato sauce, and seasonings, stir, and cook for 2 more minutes.
5. *To make custard*: While eggplant is draining, whisk together milk, egg substitute, and ½ cup Parmesan cheese in a medium saucepan. Stirring constantly, simmer over low flame for 5–7 minutes until slightly thickened and reduced by one-third. Remove from heat and set aside.
6. *To assemble*: Lightly coat a baking pan with cooking spray.
7. Rinse eggplant and pat dry. Layer ½ eggplant on bottom and top with ½ lamb-turkey mixture. Layer rest of eggplant and top with remaining lamb-turkey. Pour custard topping over the top and sprinkle it with 2 tablespoons grated Parmesan cheese.
8. Bake for 45 minutes to 1 hour or until golden.

Makes 4 servings

MOUSSAKA:
  Calories: 317.71, **Protein:** 27.16g, **Fat:** 14.62g, **Carbohydrates:** 19.14g, **Cholesterol:** 68.89mg, **Fiber:** 6.43g, **Sodium:** 344.46mg

CUSTARD TOPPING:
  Calories: 104.66, **Protein:** 11.13g, **Fat:** 5.17g, **Carbohydrates:** 7.46g, **Cholesterol:** 11.84mg, **Fiber:** 0g, **Sodium:** 335.27mg

MOUSSAKA WITH CUSTARD TOPPING:
  Calories: 422.37, **Protein:** 38.29g, **Fat:** 19.79g, **Carbohydrates:** 26.60g, **Cholesterol:** 80.73mg, **Fiber:** 6.43g, **Sodium:** 679.73mg

SERVING GUIDELINES

▶ **FOR LAP-BAND:**
  Weeks 1–4: Puree ½ cup moussaka until smooth.
  Weeks 5+: Serve ½ cup moussaka as is.

▶ **FOR BYPASS:**
  Weeks 1–4: Puree ½ cup moussaka.
  Week 5+: Serve ½ cup moussaka as is.

▶ **FOR BPD-DS:**
  Weeks 1–3: Puree ½ cup moussaka.
  Week 4+: Serve ½–1 cup moussaka as is.

▶ **FOR OTHERS:**
  Serve 1 cup moussaka as is.

Spiced Lamb Chops

This is kinda Greek, sorta Middle Eastern, but totally terrific. The spices combined with the tang of yogurt and lime really marry well with lamb.

2 garlic cloves, finely minced
¼ teaspoon ground cumin
¼ teaspoon ground
  cardamom
2 tablespoons water
1 teaspoon concentrated
  chicken broth
1 pound shoulder ½-inch-thick
  lamb chops (about 4), fat
  trimmed off
olive oil cooking spray
¾ cup plain, fat-free yogurt
1 tablespoon fresh lime juice
salt and pepper to taste

1. In a shallow plate, stir together garlic, cumin, cardamom, water, and concentrated chicken broth. Dip lamb chops in mixture, turning once to coat well. Cover with foil and marinate at room temperature for 15 minutes.

2. Coat a 12-inch nonstick skillet with cooking spray and heat skillet over medium-high heat until hot but not smoking. Remove lamb chops from marinade, reserving marinade. Cook lamb chops for about 3 minutes on each side for medium rare. Transfer lamb to a platter and keep warm.

3. Add yogurt and lime juice to reserved marinade, pour into skillet, reduce heat to low, and simmer for 2 minutes until cooked through and slightly reduced. Add salt and pepper to taste.

MAKES 4 SERVINGS

SERVING GUIDELINES

▶ **FOR LAP-BAND:**
Weeks 1–4: Puree 2 ounces cooked lamb in 2 tablespoons sauce until smooth.
Weeks 5–8: Chop 2 ounces cooked lamb and top with sauce.
Weeks 8+: Serve 2–4 ounces cooked lamb with sauce.

▶ **FOR BYPASS:**
Weeks 1–4: Puree 2 ounces cooked lamb in 2 tablespoons sauce until smooth.
Weeks 5–8: Chop 2 ounces cooked lamb and top with sauce.
Weeks 8+: Serve 2–4 ounces cooked lamb topped with sauce.

▶ **FOR BPD-DS:**
Weeks 1–3: Puree 2 ounces cooked lamb in 2 tablespoons sauce until smooth.
Weeks 4+: Serve 3–4 ounces cooked lamb topped with sauce.

▶ **FOR OTHERS:**
Serve 1 cooked lamb chop topped with sauce.

Calories: 193.93, Protein: 24.56g,
Fat: 7.77g, Carbohydrates: 4.58g,
Cholesterol: 75.78mg, Fiber: 0.10g,
Sodium: 190.60mg

Turkish Lamb and Cherry Tomatoes

IF YOU LIKE, YOU CAN MAKE THIS RECIPE ON SKEWERS AND YOU'LL HAVE SHISH KEBAB. BY MARINATING THE LAMB IN THE SPICED YOGURT, IT BECOMES INCREDIBLY TENDER.

¾ cup plain, fat-free yogurt
2 garlic cloves, finely minced
1 tablespoon tomato paste
½ teaspoon paprika
¼ teaspoon allspice
¼ teaspoon cinnamon
¼ teaspoon cumin
1 teaspoon dried thyme
¼ teaspoon cayenne pepper
1 pound lean lamb (tenderloin) cut into 1-inch cubes
24 cherry tomatoes
cooking spray
¾ cup fat-free chicken broth

1. In a large bowl, stir together yogurt, garlic, tomato paste, and spices. Reserve 2 tablespoons to make sauce.
2. Add lamb, stirring to coat. Marinate in refrigerator for 2 hours, stirring occasionally.
3. Spread lamb on broiling pan. Arrange tomatoes around lamb and spray tomatoes with cooking spray.
4. Broil lamb for about 2 minutes, then turn and broil another 2 minutes. Tomatoes should be wilted.
5. While lamb and tomatoes are cooking, combine reserved marinade with chicken broth and simmer in a small pan for 3 minutes.
6. Pour over finished lamb and serve.

MAKES 4 SERVINGS

SERVING GUIDELINES

▶ **FOR LAP-BAND:**
  Weeks 1–4: Puree 2 ounces lamb and 4 tomatoes in 2 tablespoons sauce until smooth.
  Weeks 5–8: Chop 2 ounces lamb and 4 tomatoes and top with sauce.
  Weeks 9+: Serve 2–4 ounces lamb cubes and 4 tomatoes topped with sauce.

▶ **FOR BYPASS:**
  Weeks 1–4: Puree 2 ounces lamb and 4 tomatoes in 2 tablespoons sauce until smooth.
  Weeks 5–8: Chop 2 ounces lamb and 4 tomatoes and top with sauce.
  Weeks 9+: Serve 2–4 ounces lamb cubes and 4 tomatoes topped with sauce.

▶ **FOR BPD-DS:**
  Weeks 1–3: Puree 2 ounces lamb and 4 tomatoes in 2 tablespoons sauce until smooth.
  Weeks 4+: Serve 3–4 ounces lamb cubes and 4 tomatoes topped with sauce.

▶ **FOR OTHERS:**
  Serve 4 ounces lamb cubes and 6 tomatoes topped with sauce.

Calories: 234.85, **Protein:** 29.59g, **Fat:** 7.66g, **Carbohydrates:** 11.84g, **Cholesterol:** 87.44mg, **Fiber:** 1.55g, **Sodium:** 162.04mg

Grilled Salmon with Basil Seafood Sauce

I LOVE SALMON. IT'S ONE OF THOSE WONDERFUL FISH THAT CAN STAND UP TO ANY SPICE OR ANY SAUCE. THIS RECIPE PAIRS SALMON WITH A SAUCE THAT SMOOTHLY COMBINES VERY DISTINCTIVE INGREDIENTS INTO ONE STRONG YET MELLOW FLAVOR. THE SAUCE CAN BE REFRIGERATED. IF YOU'RE LEFT WITH ANY EXTRA SAUCE, TRY MIXING IT INTO CANNED TUNA INSTEAD OF PLAIN MAYO FOR LUNCH.

olive oil cooking spray
1 pound salmon fillets
1 tablespoon light soy sauce

Basil Seafood Sauce
   (makes approximately 1 cup):
½ cup fat-free sour cream
½ cup low-fat mayonnaise
2 tablespoons prepared horse-
   radish
¼ cup fresh basil, chopped
2 teaspoons light soy sauce
2 tablespoons minced dried
   onion
1 teaspoon fresh ginger,
   minced
1 tablespoon anchovy paste

1. Spray a broiling pan with cooking spray; place salmon on pan, skin side down, and coat with cooking spray.
2. Sprinkle salmon with soy sauce and broil for 5–7 minutes until cooked through but still moist.
3. While salmon is broiling, combine all sauce ingredients in a small bowl and mix well.
4. Either pour the sauce over the finished salmon or use it for dipping.

MAKES 4 SERVINGS

SERVING GUIDELINES

▶ **FOR LAP-BAND:**
   Weeks 1–4: Puree 2 ounces cooked salmon fillet with 2 tablespoons sauce until smooth.
   Weeks 5+: Serve 2–4 ounces cooked salmon fillet topped with 2 tablespoons sauce.

▶ **FOR BYPASS:**
   Weeks 1–4: Puree 2 ounces cooked salmon fillet with 2 tablespoons sauce until smooth.
   Weeks 5+: Serve 2–4 ounces cooked salmon fillet topped with 2 tablespoons sauce.

▶ **FOR BPD-DS:**
   Weeks 1–3: Puree 2 ounces cooked salmon fillet with 2 tablespoons sauce until smooth.
   Weeks 4+: Serve 3–4 ounces cooked salmon fillet topped with 2 tablespoons sauce.

▶ **FOR OTHERS:**
   Serve 4 ounces cooked salmon fillet topped with 2 tablespoons sauce.

SALMON:
   Calories: 193.01, **Protein:** 24.41g,
   Fat: 9.71g, **Carbohydrates:** 0.25g,
   Cholesterol: 70.31mg, **Fiber:** 0g,
   Sodium: 197.05mg

BASIL SEAFOOD SAUCE (2 TABLE-SPOONS):
   Calories: 38.86, **Protein:** 1.10g,
   Fat: 3.04g, **Carbohydrates:** 2.60g,
   Cholesterol: 7.19mg, **Fiber:** 0.05g,
   Sodium: 165.77mg

Indian Spiced Salmon

THE INDIAN STYLE OF COOKING GIVES AN AUTHENTIC TOASTED SPICE FLAVOR TO THIS UNUSUAL SALMON DISH.

1 teaspoon ground coriander
1 teaspoon ground cumin
½ teaspoon ground turmeric
½ teaspoon dried thyme
½ teaspoon ground fennel
  seeds
¼ teaspoon ground black pepper
¼ teaspoon ground cinnamon
1 teaspoon ground cloves
1 pound salmon fillets
cooking spray
⅓ cup plain, fat-free yogurt

1. Mix the first 8 ingredients on a flat plate.
2. Dredge the fillets on both sides with the spice mixture, patting gently to make it stick.
3. In a large nonstick skillet, heat cooking spray just until it gets hot. Add fillets and cook about 3 minutes on each side or until medium rare. Remove the fillets and keep warm.
4. Add the yogurt to the hot pan and turn off heat. Stir to scrape up the spice flavors left in the pan.

MAKES 4 SERVINGS

Calories: 219.72, **Protein:** 26.03g, **Fat:** 10.16g, **Carbohydrates:** 3.94g, **Cholesterol:** 70.93mg, **Fiber:** 1.02g, **Sodium:** 80.48mg

SERVING GUIDELINES

▶ **FOR LAP-BAND:**
   Weeks 1–4: Puree 2 ounces cooked fish with sauce.
   Weeks 5+: Serve 2–4 ounces cooked fish topped with sauce.

▶ **FOR BYPASS:**
   Weeks 1–4: Puree 2 ounces cooked fish with sauce.
   Weeks 5+: Serve 2–4 ounces cooked fish topped with sauce.

▶ **FOR BPD-DS:**
   Weeks 1–3: Puree 2 ounces cooked fish with sauce.
   Weeks 4+: Serve 2–4 ounces cooked fish topped with sauce.

▶ **FOR OTHERS:**
   Serve 4 ounces cooked fish topped with sauce.

Salmon with Wasabi Glaze

DID YOU KNOW THAT WASABI, OFTEN CALLED JAPANESE MUSTARD, IS REALLY A HORSE-RADISH? WHATEVER YOU CALL IT, IT'S FANTASTIC WITH SALMON.

1 teaspoon wasabi paste
2 teaspoons light soy sauce
2 packets artificial sweetener
  (Splenda or Sweet 'N Low)
1 tablespoon lemon juice
1 large clove garlic, minced
cooking spray
1 pound salmon fillet

Creamy Wasabi Sauce
  (makes about ½ cup):
¼ cup fat-free sour cream
¼ cup low-fat mayonnaise
1½ teaspoons light soy sauce
½ packet artificial sweetener
1 teaspoon wasabi paste

1. In a small bowl, whisk the wasabi, soy sauce, sweetener, lemon juice, and garlic together.
2. Spray a broiling pan with cooking spray and place salmon in pan, skin side down.
3. Spread wasabi-garlic mixture on salmon fillet.
4. Broil for 7–10 minutes, depending on thickness of fish.
5. *To make wasabi sauce*: Mix all ingredients together until well blended.

MAKES 4 SERVINGS

SALMON:
  Calories: 198.90, **Protein:** 24.49g,
  Fat: 9.84g, **Carbohydrates:** 2.19g,
  Cholesterol: 70.31mg, **Fiber:**
  0.03g, **Sodium:** 168.80mg

WASABI SAUCE (2 TABLESPOONS):
  Calories: 36.59, **Protein:** 0.60g,
  Fat: 2.56g, **Carbohydrates:** 2.57g,
  Cholesterol: 3.75mg, **Fiber:** 0g,
  Sodium: 110.13mg

SERVING GUIDELINES

▶ **FOR LAP-BAND:**
  Weeks 1–4: Puree 2 ounces cooked salmon with 2 tablespoons sauce until smooth.
  Weeks 5+: Serve 2–4 ounces cooked salmon topped with 2 tablespoons sauce.

▶ **FOR BYPASS:**
  Weeks 1–4: Puree 2 ounces cooked salmon with 2 tablespoons sauce until smooth.
  Weeks 5+: Serve 2–4 ounces cooked salmon topped with 2 tablespoons sauce.

▶ **FOR BPD-DS:**
  Weeks 1–3: Puree 2 ounces cooked salmon with 2 tablespoons sauce until smooth.
  Weeks 4+: Serve 3–4 ounces cooked salmon topped with 2 tablespoons sauce.

▶ **FOR OTHERS:**
  Serve 4 ounces cooked salmon fillet topped with 2 tablespoons sauce.

Salmon with Creamy Lime-Dill Sauce

SALMON AND DILL ARE ONE OF THOSE NATURAL COMBINATIONS THAT'S SO GOOD, IT'S NEVER A CLICHÉ. OF COURSE, WE ADDED A DOLLOP OF MUSTARD TO THE SAUCE TO MAKE IT UNIQUE.

cooking spray
1 pound salmon fillet
¼ cup Dijon mustard
2 tablespoons fresh dill or 1
   tablespoon dried dill
2 tablespoons fat-free cream
   cheese
¼ cup lime juice
½ teaspoon garlic powder
½ packet artificial sweetener

1. Spray broiler pan with cooking spray. Place salmon in the pan, skin side down.
2. In a small bowl, combine ½ the mustard with 1 tablespoon dill and spread on the salmon.
3. Broil salmon for 10–12 minutes until just opaque in middle.
4. In another small bowl, combine remaining ingredients until creamy; pour over fish.

MAKES 4 SERVINGS

SERVING GUIDELINES

▶ **FOR LAP-BAND:**
   Weeks 1–4: Puree 2 ounces cooked fish with 2 tablespoons sauce.
   Weeks 5+: Serve 2–4 ounces cooked fish topped with sauce.

▶ **FOR BYPASS:**
   Weeks 1–4: Puree 2 ounces cooked fish with 2 tablespoons sauce.
   Weeks 5+: Serve 2–4 ounces cooked fish topped with sauce.

▶ **FOR BPD-DS:**
   Weeks 1–3: Puree 2 ounces cooked fish with 2 tablespoons sauce.
   Weeks 4+: Serve 2–4 ounces cooked fish topped with sauce.

▶ **FOR OTHERS:**
   Serve 4 ounces cooked fish topped with sauce.

Calories: 231.27, **Protein:** 26.52g, **Fat:** 11.17g, **Carbohydrates:** 4.86g, **Cholesterol:** 71.86mg, **Fiber:** 1.54g, **Sodium:** 174.36mg

Mustard-Crusted Halibut

USING GROUND SOY NUTS AS A COATING GIVES THIS CLASSIC RECIPE A LUSCIOUS NUTTY FLAVOR.

1 tablespoon Dijon mustard
1 tablespoon whole-grain mustard
1 teaspoon lemon rind, grated
1 teaspoon fresh thyme, chopped, or ½ teaspoons dried thyme
1 tablespoon light soy sauce
1 pound halibut fillets, skinned
½ cup ground soy nuts
1 tablespoon fresh parsley, chopped
olive oil cooking spray
1 garlic clove, minced
1 cup clam juice
salt and pepper to taste

1. In a shallow bowl, combine mustards, lemon rind, thyme, and soy sauce. Dip fish and turn to coat both sides, then remove fish (do not discard mustard mixture in bowl).
2. On a flat plate, mix ground soy nuts and parsley and dredge coated fillets in mixture, turning to coat both sides.
3. Coat a medium nonstick skillet with cooking spray and sauté fish over medium heat. Reduce heat to low and sauté for 3 minutes on each side until golden crisp and cooked through. Remove fish and keep warm.
4. Sauté garlic for 1 minute until golden. Stir in clam juice and reserved mustard mixture, scraping up any brown bits, and simmer for 3 minutes until slightly reduced.

MAKES 4 SERVINGS

SERVING GUIDELINES

▶ **FOR LAP-BAND:**
Weeks 1–4: Puree 2 ounces cooked fish with 2 tablespoons sauce.
Weeks 5+: Serve 2–4 ounces cooked fish topped with sauce.

▶ **FOR BYPASS:**
Weeks 1–4: Puree 2 ounces cooked fish with 2 tablespoons sauce.
Weeks 5+: Serve 2–4 ounces cooked fish topped with sauce.

▶ **FOR BPD-DS:**
Weeks 1–3: Puree 2 ounces cooked fish with 2 tablespoons sauce.
Weeks 4+: Serve 3–4 ounces cooked fish topped with sauce.

▶ **FOR OTHERS:**
Serve 4 ounces cooked fish topped with sauce.

Calories: 247.46, **Protein:** 32.91g, **Fat:** 8.86g, **Carbohydrates:** 8.71g, **Cholesterol:** 36.36mg, **Fiber:** 4.07g, **Sodium:** 301.76mg

Tangy Swordfish and Tomatoes

THE BEAUTY OF SWORDFISH IS THAT IT'S FLAVORFUL ENOUGH TO STAND UP TO THE MOST ASSERTIVE SAUCES, LIKE THIS ONE SPIKED WITH MUSTARD AND TARRAGON.

cooking spray
1 pound swordfish steak
1½ cups fresh tomatoes,
   chopped
2 teaspoon light soy sauce
1 tablespoon Dijon mustard
2½ teaspoons fresh tarragon or
   ¾ teaspoons dried tarragon
salt and pepper to taste

1. In a medium nonstick skillet, heat cooking spray until hot but not smoking; sear swordfish over high heat for 2 minutes on each side.
2. Reduce heat to medium and pour tomatoes around fish. Drizzle fish with soy sauce, cover, and cook for 5 minutes. Remove fish from skillet and keep warm.
3. Add mustard and tarragon to tomatoes and stir well to combine. Add salt and pepper to taste.

MAKES 4 SERVINGS

SERVING GUIDELINES

▶ **FOR LAP-BAND:**
   Weeks 1–4: Puree 2 ounces cooked fish with 2 tablespoons sauce.
   Weeks 5+: Serve 2–4 ounces cooked fish topped with sauce.

▶ **FOR BYPASS:**
   Weeks 1–4: Puree 2 ounces cooked fish with 2 tablespoons sauce.
   Weeks 5+: Serve 2–4 ounces cooked fish topped with sauce.

▶ **FOR BPD-DS:**
   Weeks 1–3: Puree 2 ounces cooked fish with 2 tablespoons sauce.
   Weeks 4+: Serve 3–4 ounces cooked fish topped with sauce.

▶ **FOR OTHERS:**
   Serve 4 ounces cooked fish topped with sauce.

Calories: 159.36, **Protein:** 23.14g, **Fat:** 5.16g, **Carbohydrates:** 4.40g, **Cholesterol:** 44.65mg, **Fiber:** 0.88g, **Sodium:** 234.91mg

Sole with White Wine and Capers

THIS SIMPLE YET ELEGANT WAY OF COOKING SOLE ALSO WORKS WITH ANY DELICATE, WHITE-FLESHED FISH, LIKE TILAPIA OR FLOUNDER.

cooking spray
¼ cup minced shallots
½ cup white wine
1 teaspoon capers
1 pound skinless sole fillets
salt and pepper to taste

1. Coat bottom of medium nonstick skillet with cooking spray; heat and sauté shallots until lightly browned.
2. Add wine and capers to pan and bring to simmer.
3. Place fish fillets in pan, cover, and poach for 3 minutes or until fish flakes easily with a fork. Add salt and pepper to taste.

MAKES 4 SERVINGS

SERVING GUIDELINES

▶ **FOR LAP-BAND:**
Weeks 1–4: Puree 2 ounces fish with 2 tablespoons sauce.
Weeks 5+: Serve 2–4 ounces fish with sauce.

▶ **FOR BYPASS:**
Weeks 1–4: Puree 2 ounces fish with 2 tablespoons sauce.
Weeks 5+: Serve 2–4 ounces fish with sauce.

▶ **FOR BPD-DS:**
Weeks 1–3: Puree 2 ounces fish with 2 tablespoons sauce.
Weeks 4+: Serve 3–4 ounces fish with sauce.

▶ **FOR OTHERS:**
Serve 4 ounces fish with sauce.

Calories: 130.45, **Protein:** 21.64g, **Fat:** 1.36g, **Carbohydrates:** 1.92g, **Cholesterol:** 54.43mg, **Fiber:** 0g, **Sodium:** 120.78mg

Bluefish with Mustard-Horseradish Glaze

YOU NEED A FISH WITH AN ASSERTIVE FLAVOR OF ITS OWN TO STAND UP TO THIS PUN-
GENT GLAZE. I THINK BLUEFISH IS PERFECT—BUT IT ALSO WORKS WITH SWORDFISH OR
SALMON. WE ADAPTED THIS RECIPE FROM *THE LEGAL SEA FOODS COOKBOOK*.

1 pound bluefish fillets
olive oil cooking spray
¼ cup light mayonnaise
1 tablespoon prepared
  horseradish
2 tablespoons Dijon mustard
¼ cup (2) minced shallots
2 teaspoons Worcestershire
  sauce
2 tablespoons minced dried
  parsley

1. Place fillets skin side down in broiling pan and coat lightly with cooking spray.
2. Place under a preheated broiler and cook 6 minutes until almost done.
3. While fish is broiling, combine mayonnaise, horseradish, mustard, shallots, Worcestershire sauce, and parsley in a small bowl.
4. Remove the fish, spread lightly with sauce, and continue broiling for about 3 minutes or until lightly browned. Sprinkle with parsley and serve.

MAKES 4 SERVINGS

SERVING GUIDELINES

▶ **FOR LAP-BAND:**
  Weeks 1–4: Puree 2 ounces
    cooked, sauced fish.
  Weeks 5+: Serve 2–4 ounces
    cooked fish as is.

▶ **FOR BYPASS:**
  Weeks 1–4: Puree 2 ounces
    cooked, sauced fish.
  Weeks 5+: Serve 2–4 ounces
    cooked fish as is.

▶ **FOR BPD-DS:**
  Weeks 1–3: Puree 2 ounces
    cooked, sauced fish.
  Weeks 4+: Serve 3–4 ounces
    cooked fish as is.

▶ **FOR OTHERS:**
  Serve 4 ounces fish as is.

Calories: 218.92, **Protein:** 25.01g, **Fat:** 11.79g, **Carbohydrates:** 5.64g, **Cholesterol:** 72.06mg, **Fiber:** 0.29g, **Sodium:** 304.59mg

Cajun-Spiced Catfish with Citrus-Horseradish Sauce

WE LOVE THE SPICINESS OF THIS FISH, ESPECIALLY WHEN IT'S CONTRASTED WITH A TANGY LEMON-LIME SAUCE.

1 pound skinless catfish fillets
2 teaspoons paprika
1 clove garlic, minced
1 teaspoon dried oregano
1 teaspoon dried thyme
½ teaspoon cayenne pepper
olive oil cooking spray

Citrus-Horseradish Sauce
   (makes a little over ½ cup):
¼ cup low-fat mayonnaise
¼ cup fat-free sour cream
1½ teaspoons fresh lemon juice
1½ teaspoons fresh lime juice
½ teaspoon lemon zest, grated
½ teaspoon lime zest, grated
1 teaspoon capers, drained
1 teaspoon prepared horseradish
¼ cup fresh basil leaves,
   chopped

1. Place fish on flat plate. Combine the next 5 ingredients thoroughly and rub on fish. Cover with foil and refrigerate for 20 minutes.
2. While fish is chilling, make the sauce: combine all sauce ingredients in a medium-sized bowl and whisk until smooth.
3. Coat a nonstick broiling pan with cooking spray, place fish on it, and broil for 4 minutes or until fish flakes easily with a fork. Serve with sauce.

MAKES 4 SERVINGS

CATFISH:
Calories: 124.94, **Protein:** 20.81g, **Fat:** 3.57g, **Carbohydrates:** 1.39g, **Cholesterol:** 65.77mg, **Fiber:** 0.43g, **Sodium:** 89.55mg

CITRUS-HORSERADISH SAUCE (2 TABLESPOONS):
Calories: 35.22, **Protein:** 0.67g, **Fat:** 2.64g, **Carbohydrates:** 2.39g, **Cholesterol:** 3.75mg, **Fiber:** 0.09g, **Sodium:** 83.84mg

SERVING GUIDELINES

▶ **FOR LAP-BAND:**
Weeks 1–4: Puree 2 ounces cooked fish with 2 tablespoons sauce.
Weeks 5+: Serve 2–4 ounces cooked fish topped with 2 tablespoons sauce.

▶ **FOR BYPASS:**
Weeks 1–4: Puree 2 ounces cooked fish with 2 tablespoons sauce.
Weeks 5+: Serve 2–4 ounces cooked fish topped with 2 tablespoons sauce.

▶ **FOR BPD-DS:**
Weeks 1–3: Puree 2 ounces cooked fish with 2 tablespoons sauce.
Weeks 4+: Serve 3–4 ounces fish topped with 2 tablespoons sauce.

▶ **FOR OTHERS:**
Serve 4 ounces fish fillet topped with 2 tablespoons sauce.

Tuna Mousse

IF YOU THINK TUNA SALAD IS BORING, WAIT'LL YOU TASTE THIS RECIPE. IT'S TERRIFIC FOR
LUNCH OR FOR A LIGHT SUMMER SUPPER.

2 6-ounce cans tuna packed in
water, drained

2 tablespoons low-fat mayonnaise

2 tablespoons fat-free sour
cream

2 tablespoons fat-free cream
cheese, softened

½ cup shallots, finely chopped

1 tablespoon fresh lemon juice

¼ teaspoon ground pepper

½ teaspoon celery seed

2 tablespoon parsley, finely
chopped

1. In a food processor, combine all ingredients except
parsley and pulse until smooth.
2. Add parsley and pulse just until combined.
3. Transfer mousse to a bowl and refrigerate for at least
1 hour before serving.

MAKES 4 SERVINGS

SERVING GUIDELINES

▶ **FOR LAP-BAND:**
Weeks 1+: Serve ¼–½ cup as is.

▶ **FOR BYPASS:**
Weeks 1+: Serve ¼–½ cup as is.

▶ **FOR BPD-DS**
Weeks 1+: Serve ¼–½ cup as is.

▶ **FOR OTHERS:**
Serve ½ cup as is.

Calories: 154.15, **Protein:** 23.37g, **Fat:** 4.25g, **Carbohydrates:** 8.79g,
Cholesterol: 5mg, **Fiber:** 0.21g, **Sodium:** 485.65mg

Balinese Shrimp

EXOTICALLY SPICED, SWEET, AND TANGY, YOU MAY BE TEMPTED TO SAVE THIS CREAMY SEAFOOD RECIPE FOR COMPANY, BUT IT'S SIMPLE ENOUGH TO PREPARE FOR A WEEKNIGHT DINNER.

cooking spray
8 garlic cloves, minced
¾ cup water
1 teaspoon ground cumin
1 teaspoon ground coriander
½ teaspoon ground turmeric
1 pound large shrimp, peeled
*   and de-veined*
1 cup plain, fat-free yogurt
2 tablespoon dried chives
2 packets artificial sweetener
*   (Splenda or Sweet 'N Low)*

1. In a large nonstick skillet, heat cooking spray until hot but not smoking. Add garlic and sauté until golden, about 30 seconds.
2. Stir in water, cumin, coriander, and turmeric; cover, reduce heat, and simmer for 7 minutes.
3. Add shrimp and cook, uncovered, stirring, for 3 minutes.
4. Stir in yogurt, chives, and sweetener and simmer over very low heat for 2 minutes, stirring occasionally.

MAKES 4 SERVINGS

SERVING GUIDELINES

▶ **FOR LAP-BAND:**
Weeks 1–4: Puree 2 ounce cooked shrimp with 2 tablespoons sauce.
Weeks 5–8: Chop 2 ounces cooked shrimp and top with sauce.
Weeks 9+: Serve 2–4 ounces cooked shrimp with sauce.

▶ **FOR BYPASS:**
Weeks 1–4: Puree 2 ounces cooked shrimp with 2 tablespoons sauce.
Weeks 5–8: Chop 2 ounces cooked shrimp and top with sauce.
Weeks 9+: Serve 2–4 ounces cooked shrimp with sauce.

▶ **FOR BPD-DS:**
Weeks 1–3: Puree 2 ounces cooked shrimp with 2 tablespoons sauce.
Weeks 4+: Serve 3–4 ounces cooked shrimp topped with sauce.

▶ **FOR OTHERS:**
Serve 4 ounces cooked shrimp topped with sauce.

Calories: 180.15, **Protein:** 27.64g, **Fat:** 2.23g, **Carbohydrates:** 10.61g, **Cholesterol:** 174.03mg, **Fiber:** 0.73, **Sodium:** 233.71mg

Chilled Shrimp with Ponzu Sauce

PONZU, THE TRADITIONAL CHINESE SAUCE, GIVES THIS LIGHT SUMMERY DISH A SWEETLY SPICY KICK.

1 pound large shrimp, shelled and de-veined

2 tablespoons light soy sauce

2 tablespoons orange juice

2 tablespoons lime juice

brown-sugar artificial sweetener (2 teaspoons equivalent)

½ teaspoon Asian chili paste with garlic

1 tablespoon fresh ginger, finely minced

¼ cup chopped fresh basil

SERVING GUIDELINES

▶ **FOR LAP-BAND:**
Weeks 1–4: Puree 2 ounces cooked shrimp with 2 tablespoons sauce.
Weeks 5–8: Chop 2 ounces cooked shrimp with sauce.
Weeks 9+: Serve 2–4 ounces cooked shrimp with sauce.

▶ **FOR BYPASS:**
Weeks 1–4: Puree 2 ounces cooked shrimp with 2 tablespoons sauce.
Weeks 5–8: Chop 2 ounces cooked shrimp with sauce.
Weeks 9+: Serve 2–4 ounces cooked shrimp with sauce.

▶ **FOR BPD-DS:**
Weeks 1–3: Puree 2 ounces cooked shrimp with 2 tablespoons sauce.
Weeks 4+: Serve 3–4 ounces cooked shrimp with sauce.

▶ **FOR OTHERS:**
Serve 4 ounces cooked shrimp with sauce.

1. In a large pot, bring 4 quarts of water to a rapid boil, add shrimp, and cook for 1 minute.
2. Drain shrimp and immediately transfer to a bowl of ice water. When chilled, drain shrimp and refrigerate.
3. *To make Ponzu sauce*: In a small bowl, combine all other ingredients. (Sauce can be refrigerated until ready to use, up to 10 hours.) Toss shrimp with sauce 10 minutes before serving.

MAKES 4 SERVINGS

Calories: 139.70, **Protein:** 24g, **Fat:** 2.01g, **Carbohydrates:** 3.80g, **Cholesterol:** 173.37mg, **Fiber:** 0.26g, **Sodium:** 447.55mg

Shrimp Calypso

Tangy with a creamy yogurt and pineapple sauce, this recipe gets its tropical heat from typical island spicing. This dish can be served hot or cold.

1 pound large shrimp, shelled
  and de-veined
1 teaspoon crushed red pepper
1 teaspoon turmeric
1 teaspoon fresh ginger, peeled
  and grated
2 garlic cloves, minced
1 cup plain, fat-free yogurt
½ cup green onions (scallions),
  chopped
½ cup fresh pineapple, diced
1 tablespoon fresh cilantro,
  chopped
cooking spray

1. Combine shrimp and next 6 ingredients in a large zip-top plastic bag. Seal and turn to coat all shrimp, then marinate in refrigerator for 30 minutes.
2. Pour shrimp and marinade into a large skillet and cook over medium heat, stirring, for 3 minutes.
3. Stir in pineapple and cook 2 minutes. Sprinkle with cilantro and serve.

Makes 4 servings

SERVING GUIDELINES

▶ **FOR LAP-BAND:**
  Weeks 1–4: Puree 2 ounces cooked shrimp with 2 tablespoon sauce.
  Weeks 5–8: Chop 2 ounces cooked shrimp and top with sauce.
  Weeks 9+: Serve 2–4 ounces cooked shrimp with sauce.

▶ **FOR BYPASS:**
  Weeks 1–4: Puree 2 ounces cooked shrimp with 2 tablespoons sauce.
  Weeks 5–8: Chop 2 ounces cooked shrimp and top with sauce.
  Weeks 9+: Serve 2–4 ounces cooked shrimp with sauce.

▶ **FOR BPD-DS:**
  Weeks 1–3: Puree 2 ounces cooked shrimp with 2 tablespoons sauce.
  Weeks 4+: Serve 3–4 ounces cooked shrimp topped with sauce.

▶ **FOR OTHERS:**
  Serve 4 ounces cooked shrimp topped with sauce.

Calories: 184.25, **Protein:** 27.54g,
Fat: 2.21g, **Carbohydrates:** 11.77g,
Cholesterol: 174.03mg, **Fiber:** 0.74g,
Sodium: 234.11mg

Shrimp Italiano

THIS RECIPE IS BASED ON ONE THAT I HAVE BEEN MAKING FOR YEARS—ITALIAN VEGETABLE STEW. IT'S SORT OF LIKE A FRENCH ratatouille WITHOUT THE EGGPLANT. IT CAN BE SERVED HOT OR COLD.

olive oil cooking spray

¾ cup onions, coarsely chopped

3 large cloves of garlic, minced

½ pound fresh white mushrooms, cut into eighths

1 cup (1 small) zucchini, cut coarsely into cubes

1 cup bell pepper, seeded and cut up coarsely

1 14.5-ounce can of diced tomatoes

¼ cup of dry red wine

1½ teaspoons fresh basil, minced, or ¾ teaspoons dried basil

½ teaspoon hot pepper flakes

1 pound large shrimp, cleaned and peeled

salt and pepper to taste

1. Coat bottom of large cooking pot with cooking spray and sauté onions, garlic, and mushrooms over medium heat for 5–7 minutes until just translucent.
2. Add all other ingredients except the shrimp. Cover pot and cook over low flame for 2 hours.
3. Add shrimp, cover pot, and simmer for 3 minutes until shrimp turn pink. Add salt and pepper to taste.

MAKES 4 SERVINGS

Calories: 219.27, **Protein:** 27.64g, **Fat:** 2.37g, **Carbohydrates:** 17.36g, **Cholesterol:** 172.37mg, **Fiber:** 4.07g, **Sodium:** 334.66mg

SERVING GUIDELINES

▶ **FOR LAP-BAND:**
Weeks 1–4: Puree 2 ounces cooked shrimp with ¼ cup vegetables.
Weeks 5–8: Chop 2 ounces cooked shrimp and serve with ¼ cup vegetables.
Weeks 9+: Serve 2–4 ounces shrimp with ¼ cup vegetables.

▶ **FOR BYPASS:**
Weeks 1–4: Puree 2 ounces cooked shrimp with ¼ cup vegetables.
Weeks 5–8: Chop 2 ounces cooked shrimp and serve with ¼ cup vegetables.
Weeks 9+: Serve 2–4 ounces shrimp with ¼ cup vegetables.

▶ **FOR BPD-DS:**
Weeks 1–3: Puree 2 ounces cooked shrimp with ¼ cup vegetables.
Weeks 4+: Serve 3–4 ounces shrimp with ½ cup vegetables.

▶ **FOR OTHERS:**
Serve 4 ounces shrimp with ½–1 cup vegetables.

Shrimp Scampi

For those of you who think that scampi without lots of olive oil or butter isn't possible, try this recipe. It has all the flavor of a traditional scampi, but it's lighter and brighter.

olive oil cooking spray
½ cup minced shallots
3 garlic cloves, minced
1 pound large shrimp, peeled
* and de-veined*
½ cup white wine
¼ cup clam juice
¼ cup fresh parsley, chopped
2 tablespoons fresh lemon juice
salt and pepper to taste

SERVING GUIDELINES

▶ **FOR LAP-BAND:**
  Weeks 1–4: Puree 2 ounces cooked shrimp with 2 table-spoons sauce.
  Weeks 5–8: Chop 2 ounces cooked shrimp with sauce.
  Weeks 9+: Serve 2–4 ounces cooked shrimp with sauce.

▶ **FOR BYPASS:**
  Weeks 1–4: Puree 2 ounces cooked shrimp with 2 table-spoons sauce.
  Weeks 5–8: Chop 2 ounces cooked shrimp with sauce.
  Weeks 9+: Serve 2–4 ounces cooked shrimp with sauce.

▶ **FOR BPD-DS:**
  Weeks 1–3: Puree 2 ounces cooked shrimp with 2 table-spoons sauce.
  Weeks 4+: Serve 3–4 ounces cooked shrimp topped with sauce.

▶ **FOR OTHERS:**
  Serve 4 ounces cooked shrimp topped with sauce.

1. In a large nonstick skillet, heat cooking spray until hot but not smoking. Sauté shallots and garlic for 1 minute until barely golden.
2. Add shrimp and sauté until they just turn pink.
3. Stir in wine and clam juice and bring to a boil. Reduce heat to medium and cook 30 seconds.
4. Add parsley and lemon juice. Toss well to coat shrimp and cook for 1 minute. Add salt and pepper to taste.

Makes 4 servings

Calories: 161.94, **Protein:** 24.01g, **Fat:** 2.03g, **Carbohydrates:** 6.27g, **Cholesterol:** 172.37mg, **Fiber:** 0.20g, **Sodium:** 192.60mg

Shrimp with Coconut-Curry Tomato Sauce

HERE'S A CREAMY, SPICY SHRIMP CURRY THAT'S SO FULL OF AUTHENTIC FLAVOR, IT'S HARD TO BELIEVE THAT WE'RE ALLOWED TO EAT IT.

cooking spray (canola oil)
½ cup onion, sliced thin
3 garlic cloves, minced
1 small jalapeño chili, seeded and chopped
½ tablespoon fresh ginger, minced
1½ teaspoons mild curry powder
1 28-ounce can diced tomatoes
1 14-ounce can light unsweetened coconut milk
1 packet artificial sweetener (Splenda or Sweet 'N Low)
1 pound fresh large shrimp, shelled and de-veined

1. In a large nonstick skillet, heat cooking spray until hot but not smoking. Sauté onion, garlic, jalapeño, and ginger about 5 minutes, until soft. Add curry powder and cook until fragrant, about 30 seconds.
2. Add tomatoes with their juice, coconut milk, and artificial sweetener. Simmer over low heat for about 15 minutes, until slightly thickened.
3. Add shrimp and cook, stirring, for 3–5 minutes, until shrimps turn pink and opaque.

MAKES 4 SERVINGS

Calories: 284.10, **Protein:** 26.71g, **Fat:** 9.12g, **Carbohydrates:** 20.41g, **Cholesterol:** 172.37mg, **Fiber:** 3.98g, **Sodium:** 504.30mg

SERVING GUIDELINES

▶ **FOR LAP-BAND:**
 Weeks 1–4: Puree 2 ounces cooked shrimp with 2 tablespoons sauce.
 Weeks 5–8: Chop 2 ounces cooked shrimp and top with sauce.
 Weeks 9+: Serve 2–4 ounces cooked shrimp with sauce.

▶ **FOR BYPASS:**
 Weeks 1–4: Puree 2 ounces cooked shrimp with 2 tablespoons sauce.
 Weeks 5–8: Chop 2 ounces cooked shrimp and top with sauce.
 Weeks 9+: Serve 2–4 ounces cooked shrimp with sauce.

▶ **FOR BPD-DS:**
 Weeks 1–3: Puree 2 ounces cooked shrimp with 2 tablespoons sauce.
 Weeks 4+: Serve 2–4 ounces cooked shrimp with sauce.

▶ **FOR OTHERS:**
 Serve 4 ounces cooked shrimp topped with sauce.

Singapore Shrimp Dumplings

EVEN THOUGH THESE DELICATE DUMPLINGS USE CABBAGE LEAVES INSTEAD OF TRADITIONAL DOUGH WRAPPERS, THEY REALLY TASTE AUTHENTIC, NOT TO MENTION DELICIOUS.

1 pound large shrimp, shelled and de-veined

1 10-ounce package frozen chopped spinach, thawed and squeezed dry

½ cup scallions, chopped

2 teaspoons Asian chili paste with garlic

2 teaspoons fresh ginger, grated

1 teaspoon sesame oil

2 packets artificial sweetener (Splenda or Sweet 'N Low)

2 teaspoons dry sherry

2 teaspoons light soy sauce

½ pound (8 large) cabbage leaves, steamed until soft

2 cups water

Asian dipping sauce

(makes approximately 1 cup):

¾ cup light soy sauce

¼ cup rice vinegar

2 teaspoons red pepper flakes or to taste

1 teaspoon sesame oil

brown-sugar artificial sweetener (1 teaspoon equivalent)

DUMPLINGS:
Calories: 176.13, **Protein:** 26.42g, **Fat:** 3.21g, **Carbohydrates:** 9.07g, **Cholesterol:** 172.37mg, **Fiber:** 5.08g, **Sodium:** 364.56mg

DIPPING SAUCE (2 TABLESPOONS):
Calories: 14.77, **Protein:** 1.25g, **Fat:** 0.36g, **Carbohydrates:** 1.74g, **Cholesterol:** 0mg, **Fiber:** 0.06g, **Sodium:** 406.57mg

1. In food processor, pulse shrimp to a coarse paste.
2. In a bowl, mix shrimp with spinach, scallions, chili paste, ginger, sesame oil, sweetener, sherry, and soy sauce until well combined.
3. *To make dumplings:* Lay 1 cabbage leaf on flat surface like a countertop or cutting board. Cut rib from center of leaf. In the middle of leaf half, mound 1 heaping tablespoon of shrimp mixture. Fold top and bottom of leaf over filling, then fold in sides of leaf (you may need a toothpick to hold closed). Repeat process until all leaves are filled.
4. In a large pot or skillet, bring water to a boil. Place a steamer insert in pot and arrange dumplings in steamer. Cover and steam for 8–10 minutes.
5. In a small bowl, combine all dipping sauce ingredients.

MAKES 4 SERVINGS (16 DUMPLINGS)

SERVING GUIDELINES

▶ **FOR LAP-BAND:**
Weeks 1–4: Puree 2 steamed dumplings with 2 tablespoons sauce.
Week 5+: Serve 2–4 steamed dumplings as is with sauce.

▶ **FOR BYPASS:**
Weeks 1–4: Puree 2 steamed dumplings with 2 tablespoons sauce.
Week 5+: Serve 2–4 steamed dumplings as is with sauce.

▶ **FOR BPD-DS:**
Weeks 1–3: Puree 2 steamed dumplings with 2 tablespoons sauce.
Week 4+: Serve 3–4 steamed dumplings with sauce.

▶ **FOR OTHERS:**
Serve 4 dumplings with sauce.

Asian Marinated Scallops

THIS IS A LIGHT WAY TO TREAT THE DELICATE FLAVOR OF SCALLOPS—A LIVELY CITRUS MARINADE WITH DELICIOUS CHINESE ACCENTS.

1 pound (about 12) sea scallops

Marinade:
½ cup low-sodium soy sauce
¼ teaspoon fresh lime juice
¼ teaspoon orange juice
¼ teaspoon fresh lemon juice
brown-sugar artificial sweetener (1½ teaspoons equivalent)
1 tablespoon fresh ginger, finely grated
1 teaspoon Asian sesame oil
cooking spray

1. In a wide shallow bowl, combine the marinade ingredients and mix well.
2. Add scallops and marinate at room temperature for 5 minutes (2½ minutes on each side). Do not marinate any longer or scallops will turn soft. Transfer scallops to a plate and reserve the marinade.
3. Heat cooking spray in a large nonstick skillet until hot but not smoking. Sauté scallops 2 minutes on each side until golden brown and just cooked through. Transfer to a plate.
4. Add the marinade to the skillet and boil over medium-high heat until reduced to about half (¼ cup).

MAKES 4 SERVINGS

SERVING GUIDELINES

▶ **FOR LAP-BAND:**
Weeks 1–4: Puree 2 cooked scallops with 1 tablespoon sauce.
Weeks 5–8: Chop 2 cooked scallops and top with sauce.
Weeks 9+: Serve 2–3 cooked scallops with sauce.

▶ **FOR BYPASS:**
Weeks 1–4: Puree 2 cooked scallops with 1 tablespoon sauce.
Weeks 5–8: Chop 2 cooked scallops and top with sauce.
Weeks 9+: Serve 2–3 cooked scallops with sauce.

▶ **FOR BPD-DS:**
Weeks 1–3: Puree 2 cooked scallops with 1 tablespoon sauce.
Weeks 4+: Serve 2–3 cooked scallops with sauce.

▶ **FOR OTHERS:**
Serve 3 cooked scallops with sauce.

Calories: 146.15, **Protein:** 22.29g, **Fat:** 2.11g, **Carbohydrates:** 7.07g, **Cholesterol:** 37.42mg, **Fiber:** 0g, **Sodium:** 1,266.58mg

Coquilles Saint-Jacques

THIS UPDATED CLASSIC IS PROOF THAT YOU DON'T NEED CREAM OR BUTTER TO MAKE AN INCREDIBLY RICH-TASTING DISH.

1 pound (about 12) sea scallops
cooking spray
3 pinches crumbled saffron
¼ cup shallots, finely minced
1 tablespoon white wine
1 tablespoon dry vermouth
½ cup clam juice
½ cup evaporated skim milk

SERVING GUIDELINES

► **FOR LAP-BAND:**
Weeks 1–4: Puree 2 cooked scallops with 2 tablespoons sauce.
Weeks 5–8: Chop 2 cooked scallops and top with sauce.
Weeks 9+: Serve 2–3 cooked scallops with sauce.

► **FOR BYPASS:**
Weeks 1–4: Puree 2 cooked scallops with 2 tablespoons sauce.
Weeks 5–8: Chop 2 cooked scallops and top with sauce.
Weeks 9+: Serve 2–3 cooked scallops with sauce.

► **FOR BPD-DS:**
Weeks 1–3: Puree 2 cooked scallops with 2 tablespoons sauce.
Weeks 4+: Serve 2–3 cooked scallops with sauce.

► **FOR OTHERS:**
Serve 3 cooked scallops with sauce.

1. Pat scallops dry and remove tough muscle from side of each scallop, if necessary.
2. Coat a large nonstick skillet with cooking spray. Sprinkle pan with a pinch of saffron and heat until moderately hot but not smoking.
3. Add scallops in a single layer and cook them undisturbed over medium-high heat for 2 minutes on each side, until golden and just cooked through. Remove scallops and keep warm.
4. Re-spray pan, sprinkle with remaining saffron, and reduce heat to low. Cook shallots, stirring until soft.
5. Add wine and vermouth to de-glaze skillet, scraping up any brown bits. Raise heat to medium-high, add clam juice, and boil until liquid is reduced by half.
6. Add evaporated milk and any scallop juices that have accumulated. Reduce heat and simmer until reduced to a thickened, creamy consistency.

MAKES 4 SERVINGS

Calories: 142.38, **Protein:** 21.64g, **Fat:** 0.88g, **Carbohydrates:** 8.58g, **Cholesterol:** 37.42mg, **Fiber:** 0.01g, **Sodium:** 261.07mg

Scallops Piquant

An easy yet elegant way to prepare scallops. Reducing the mustard-wine sauce gives it a lush, creamy consistency.

olive oil cooking spray
1 pound (about 12) sea scallops,
tough side muscle removed (if
necessary)
½ cup minced shallots
½ cup white wine
½ cup water
¼ cup Dijon mustard

1. Heat cooking spray in a large nonstick skillet until hot but not smoking. Sauté scallops for 1–2 minutes on each side (depending on size) until golden and just cooked through. Remove and keep warm.
2. Re-spray skillet and cook shallots over medium heat, stirring, for 1 minute until softened.
3. Add wine and boil, then cook, scraping up any brown bits, for 1 minute. Stir in water and mustard, reduce heat, and simmer 7–8 minutes until liquid is reduced to about ¾ cup.

Makes 4 servings

SERVING GUIDELINES

▶ **FOR LAP-BAND:**
Weeks 1–4: Puree 2 cooked scallops with 2 tablespoons sauce.
Weeks 5–8: Chop 2 cooked scallops and top with sauce.
Weeks 9+: Serve 2–3 cooked scallops with sauce.

▶ **FOR BYPASS:**
Weeks 1–4: Puree 2 cooked scallops with 2 tablespoons sauce.
Weeks 5–8: Chop 2 cooked scallops and top with sauce.
Weeks 9+: Serve 2–3 cooked scallops with sauce.

▶ **FOR BPD-DS:**
Weeks 1–3: Puree 2 cooked scallops with 2 tablespoons sauce.
Weeks 4+: Serve 2–3 cooked scallops with sauce.

▶ **FOR OTHERS:**
Serve 3 cooked scallops with sauce.

Calories: 153.45, **Protein:** 20.52g, **Fat:** 2.02g, **Carbohydrates:** 7.89g, **Cholesterol:** 37.72mg, **Fiber:** 0.27g, **Sodium:** 271.65mg

Scallops Provençale

THIS LUSCIOUS CLASSIC DISH IS FULL OF THE BRIGHT SUMMERY FLAVORS OF FRESH BASIL AND RIPE TOMATOES.

1 pound (about 12) large sea scallops, patted dry
olive oil cooking spray
4 garlic cloves, sliced thin
1½ cups fresh tomatoes, seeded and diced
⅛ teaspoon dried thyme
¼ cup fresh basil, shredded
½ cup dry white wine

SERVING GUIDELINES

▶ **FOR LAP-BAND:**
  Weeks 1–4: Puree 3 scallop halves with 2 tablespoons of tomato-wine mixture.
  Weeks 5–8: Chop 3 scallop halves and top with tomato-wine mixture.
  Weeks 9+: Serve 3–6 scallop halves topped with tomato-wine mixture.

▶ **FOR BYPASS:**
  Weeks 1–4: Puree 3 scallop halves with 2 tablespoons of tomato-wine mixture.
  Weeks 5–8: Chop 3 scallop halves, and top with tomato-wine mixture.
  Weeks 9+: Serve 3–6 scallop halves topped with tomato-wine mixture.

▶ **FOR BPD-DS:**
  Weeks 1–3: Puree 3 scallop halves with 2 tablespoons of tomato-wine mixture.
  Weeks 4+: Serve 3–6 scallop halves topped with tomato-wine mixture.

▶ **FOR OTHERS:**
  Serve 6 scallop halves with tomato-wine mixture.

1. Slice the scallops in half horizontally, removing the tough outer muscle, if necessary.
2. In a nonstick skillet large enough to hold the scallops in one layer, heat cooking spray until it is hot but not smoking. Sear scallops for 1–2 minutes on each side until they are golden brown and just cooked through. Use a slotted spoon to transfer scallops to a platter and cover loosely to keep warm.
3. Re-spray pan and cook garlic over moderate heat, stirring until it is lightly browned.
4. Add the tomatoes, thyme, and basil and cook mixture, stirring, for 1 minute.
5. Add wine and stir for 1 minute. Reduce heat and simmer about 5 minutes until tomatoes are soft and sauce is slightly thickened.

MAKES 4 SERVINGS

Calories: 139.75, **Protein:** 19.89g, **Fat:** 1.12g, **Carbohydrates:** 7.17g, **Cholesterol:** 37.42mg, **Fiber:** 0.92g, **Sodium:** 190.75mg

Scallops with White Wine and Garlic

THIS DISH COULDN'T BE SIMPLER TO MAKE, AND THE GARLIC SEEMS TO INTENSIFY THE SWEET SCALLOP FLAVOR.

olive oil cooking spray
1 pound (about 12) sea scallops,
sliced in half horizontally
8 cloves of garlic, minced
¾ cup white wine
¼ cup fresh parsley, minced, or
3 tablespoons dried parsley

1. In a nonstick skillet large enough to hold all scallops in 1 layer, heat cooking spray until hot but not smoking. Add scallops, sprinkle with garlic, and brown well on 1 side (2–3 minutes).
2. Turn scallops and brown well on other side (garlic should get brown and crunchy). Remove scallops from pan and keep warm.
3. De-glaze pan with white wine, scraping up any brown bits and garlic.
4. Add parsley and simmer uncovered for 5 minutes.

MAKES 4 SERVINGS

SERVING GUIDELINES

▶ **FOR LAP-BAND:**
   Weeks 1–4: Puree 3 cooked scallop halves with 2 tablespoons sauce.
   Weeks 5–8: Chop 3 cooked scallop halves and top with sauce.
   Weeks 9+: Serve 3–6 cooked scallop halves with sauce.

▶ **FOR BYPASS:**
   Weeks 1–4: Puree 3 cooked scallop halves with 2 tablespoons sauce.
   Weeks 5–8: Chop 3 cooked scallop halves and top with sauce.
   Weeks 9+: Serve 3–6 cooked scallop halves with sauce.

▶ **FOR BPD-DS:**
   Weeks 1–3: Puree 3 cooked scallop halves with 2 tablespoons sauce.
   Weeks 4+: Serve 3–6 cooked scallop halves with sauce.

▶ **FOR OTHERS:**
   Serve 6 cooked scallop halves with sauce.

Calories: 140.17, **Protein:** 19.56g, **Fat:** 0.93g, **Carbohydrates:** 5.25g, **Cholesterol:** 37.42mg, **Fiber:** 0.24g, **Sodium:** 187.91mg

Orange-Ginger Tofu

THIS IS A LIGHT AND REFRESHING CHINESE-INFLUENCED RECIPE THAT'S JUST AS TASTY SERVED HOT AS IT IS COLD. IF YOU WANT A TRULY VEGETARIAN DISH, YOU CAN SUBSTITUTE VEGETABLE BROTH FOR THE CHICKEN BROTH, BUT REMEMBER, IT MAY CHANGE THE NUTRITIONAL ANALYSIS NUMBERS.

½ cup orange juice

1 tablespoon orange zest

1 cup fat-free, low-sodium chicken broth

1 tablespoon dry sherry

brown-sugar artificial sweetener (1 teaspoon equivalent)

1 tablespoon sesame oil

cooking spray

1 tablespoon fresh ginger, minced

2 large garlic cloves, minced

1½ cups (2 large) leeks, sliced thin

1 pound firm tofu, drained and cubed

1. Combine orange juice, zest, chicken broth, sherry, sweetener, and sesame oil in a small bowl and set aside.
2. Heat cooking spray in a medium nonstick skillet until hot but not smoking. Stir-fry ginger and garlic for 30 seconds. Add leeks and stir-fry for 3 minutes.
3. Add tofu and stir-fry for 4 minutes. Remove tofu-vegetable mixture from pan.
4. Pour orange juice mixture into pan, bring to a boil, reduce heat, and cook for 10 minutes or until reduced by half.
5. Stir in tofu-vegetable mixture and simmer for 1 minute.

MAKES 4 SERVINGS

SERVING GUIDELINES

▶ **FOR LAP-BAND:**
Weeks 1–4: Puree ¼–1/2 cup tofu mixture until smooth.
Weeks 5–8: Chop ¼–½ cup tofu mixture.
Weeks 9+: Serve ½–¾ cup tofu mixture as is.

▶ **FOR BYPASS:**
Weeks 1–4: Puree ¼–½ cup tofu mixture until smooth.
Weeks 5–8: Chop ¼–½ cup tofu mixture.
Weeks 9+: Serve ½–¾ cup tofu mixture as is.

▶ **FOR BPD-DS:**
Weeks 1–3: Puree ¼–½ cup tofu mixture until smooth.
Weeks 4+: Serve ½–1 cup tofu mixture as is.

▶ **FOR OTHERS:**
Serve 1 cup tofu mixture as is.

Calories: 250.18, **Protein:** 19.88g, **Fat:** 13.76g, **Carbohydrates:** 14.40g, **Cholesterol:** 0mg, **Fiber:** 3.42g, **Sodium:** 41.15mg

Tofu and Vegetable Curry

THIS IS A CLASSIC VEGETABLE CURRY—WE JUST ADDED SOME TOFU FOR PROTEIN. IF YOU LIKE YOUR CURRY HOTTER, YOU CAN INCREASE THE CURRY PASTE OR THROW IN SOME MINCED HOT PEPPERS.

1 cup light unsweetened coconut milk

3 packets artificial sweetener (Splenda or Sweet 'N Low)

2 tablespoons light soy sauce

1½ tablespoons fresh ginger, grated

2 cloves garlic, minced

1 teaspoon green curry paste

cooking spray

1 pound extra-firm tofu, drained and cut into 1-inch cubes

1 cup red bell pepper, cut into strips

4 cups shredded cabbage

1 cup fat-free, low-sodium vegetable broth

1 cup scallions, chopped

3 tablespoon fresh cilantro, chopped

1. In a small bowl, combine coconut milk, sweetener, soy sauce, ginger, garlic, and curry paste
2. In a large nonstick skillet; heat cooking spray until hot but not smoking. Add tofu and sauté for 10 minutes, stirring occasionally or until golden brown. Remove from pan and keep warm.
3. Add bell pepper to pan and sauté for 1 minute. Add cabbage and broth, lower heat, cover, and simmer for 15 minutes.
4. Stir in coconut milk mixture, scallions, cilantro, and tofu and cook for 2 minutes.

MAKES 4 SERVINGS

SERVING GUIDELINES

▶ **FOR LAP-BAND:**
Weeks 1–4: Puree ¼–½ cup curry until smooth.
Weeks 5–8: Chop ¼–½ cup curry.
Weeks 9+: Serve ½–¾ cup curry as is.

▶ **FOR BYPASS:**
Weeks 1–4: Puree ¼–½ cup curry until smooth.
Weeks 5–8: Chop ¼–½ cup curry.
Weeks 9+: Serve ½–¾ cup curry as is.

▶ **FOR BPD-DS:**
Weeks 1–3: Puree ¼–½ cup curry until smooth.
Weeks 4+: Serve ½–1 cup curry as is.

▶ **FOR OTHERS:**
Serve 1 cup curry as is.

Calories: 273.05, **Protein:** 21.12g, **Fat:** 14.60g, **Carbohydrates:** 18.23g, **Cholesterol:** 0mg, **Fiber:** 5.75g, **Sodium:** 602.32mg

Tofu Mexicano

IF YOU'RE INTO TEX-MEX FLAVORS, THIS DISH HAS IT ALL. HERE'S A SERVING IDEA: ONCE YOU'RE EATING SOLID FOOD, TRY SPOONING EACH PORTION ONTO LETTUCE LEAVES AND WRAPPING IT LIKE A TORTILLA.

cooking spray
2 cups onion, chopped
1 large clove garlic, minced
½ teaspoon ground cumin
½ teaspoon chili powder
1 pound extra-firm tofu, drained and cubed
1 cup bell pepper, seeded and chopped
1 small jalapeño pepper, seeded and chopped
1 cup tomatoes, chopped
½ cup low-fat cheddar cheese, shredded
salt and pepper to taste

1. Heat cooking spray in a large nonstick ovenproof skillet until hot but not smoking. Cook onion, garlic, cumin, and chili powder for 3 minutes until onion is softened.
2. Add tofu, bell pepper, jalapeño, and tomatoes and cook about 3 minutes until peppers are softened.
3. Sprinkle cheese on top and place under broiler for 40 seconds or until cheese melts and becomes bubbly. Add salt and pepper to taste.

MAKES 4 SERVINGS

Calories: 308.84, **Protein:** 26.72g, **Fat:** 16.37g, **Carbohydrates:** 16.97g, **Cholesterol:** 20mg, **Fiber:** 5.53g, **Sodium:** 266.99mg

SERVING GUIDELINES

▶ **FOR LAP-BAND:**
Weeks 1–4: Puree ¼–½ cup tofu mixture until smooth.
Weeks 5–8: Chop ¼–½ cup tofu mixture.
Weeks 9+: Serve ½–¾ cup tofu mixture as is.

▶ **FOR BYPASS:**
Weeks 1–4: Puree ¼–½ cup tofu mixture until smooth.
Weeks 5–8: Chop ¼–½ cup tofu mixture.
Weeks 9+: Serve ½–¾ cup tofu mixture as is.

▶ **FOR BPD-DS:**
Weeks 1–3: Puree ¼–½ cup tofu mixture until smooth.
Weeks 4+: Serve ½–1 cup tofu mixture as is.

▶ **FOR OTHERS:**
Serve 1 cup tofu mixture as is.

Tofu Tikka

INSTEAD OF MAKING THE USUAL TIKKA WITH CHICKEN, WE DECIDED TO SUBSTITUTE TOFU. WHEN THE TOFU IS MARINATED, IT REALLY TAKES ON ALL THE SPICE AND FLAVORS, SO IT SEEMS TO EXPLODE IN YOUR MOUTH.

1 large clove garlic, chopped
½ teaspoon fresh ginger, grated
½ small red chili, seeded
½ teaspoon cumin
½ teaspoon ground coriander
½ teaspoon turmeric
½ teaspoon garam masala
1 cup plain, fat-free yogurt
2 tablespoons lime juice
1 pound extra-firm tofu, drained and quartered
cooking spray
½ cup fat-free, low-sodium vegetable broth

1. In a food processor, combine garlic, ginger, and chili and process until finely chopped. Add cumin, coriander, turmeric, garam masala, yogurt, and lime juice and blend to make a smooth paste.
2. Place yogurt mixture in shallow bowl and add tofu, stirring to coat completely. Cover bowl and chill in refrigerator for at least 4 hours.
3. Twenty minutes before cooking, remove tofu from refrigerator and allow to become room temperature. Remove tofu from marinade and scrape off excess, reserving marinade.
4. Coat a large nonstick skillet with cooking spray and sauté tofu over medium-high heat, turning once or twice, for 15–20 minutes, until nicely browned. Remove tofu from pan and cut into 1-inch cubes.
5. Over medium-low heat, de-glaze pan with vegetable broth, scraping up any brown bits. Add reserved marinade and tofu and simmer for 3 minutes.

MAKES 4 SERVINGS

SERVING GUIDELINES

▶ **FOR LAP-BAND:**
Weeks 1–4: Puree ¼–½ cup tofu mixture until smooth.
Weeks 5–8: Chop ¼–½ cup tofu mixture.
Weeks 9+: Serve ½–¾ cup tofu mixture as is.

▶ **FOR BYPASS:**
Weeks 1–4: Puree ¼–½ cup tofu mixture until smooth.
Weeks 5–8: Chop ¼–½ cup tofu mixture.
Weeks 9+: Serve ½–¾ cup tofu mixture as is.

▶ **FOR BPD-DS:**
Weeks 1–3: Puree ¼–½ cup tofu mixture until smooth.
Weeks 4+: Serve ½–1 cup tofu mixture as is.

▶ **FOR OTHERS:**
Serve 1 cup tofu mixture as is.

Calories: 218.19, **Protein:** 22.40g, **Fat:** 10.19g, **Carbohydrates:** 13.16g, **Cholesterol:** 1.67mg, **Fiber:** 3.08g, **Sodium:** 205.44mg

Sweet Indulgences

SINCE WE DESIGNED this cookbook to be used not just in those first weeks after surgery, but for the months and years after, we knew that we had to include some really great sweets. Let's face it: you can deny your sweet cravings for a while, but not for the rest of your life.

Can you really have desserts? Yes, if they are low-fat, high-protein desserts like the recipes we provide you with here, which are made with no added sugars. They are so delicious even your "others" will enjoy them.

You might be wondering now that you have to eat so much less, if you will even have room for dessert after a meal. That's a valid concern. You might not be able to eat these dishes directly after a meal, but your nutritionist has probably told you that you can eat one healthy snack during the day. These recipes make perfect snacks—for example, Strawberry Ricotta Whip or one of our fresh fruit-and-yogurt smoothies. We've even included a delicious low-fat hot chocolate.

So go ahead, indulge. After all, your surgery didn't remove your sweet tooth.

Note: The nutritional analyses are based on an average portion size (*Others'* portions).

Desserts and beverages that taste too good to be true— but they are

Basic Cheesecake

THIS IS A LIGHT, ALMOST FLUFFY CHEESECAKE THAT LITERALLY MELTS IN YOUR MOUTH.

*1 8-ounce container fat-free
  cream cheese*
½ pound soft tofu
½ cup egg substitute
*6 packets artificial sweetener
  (Splenda or Sweet 'N Low)*
½ teaspoon vanilla
¼ teaspoon almond extract
*6 tablespoons egg white substi-
  tute*
¼ teaspoon cream of tartar
butter-flavored cooking spray

1. Preheat oven to 350°F.
2. In a large bowl, using an electric mixer, beat together cream cheese, tofu, egg substitute, sweetener, vanilla, and almond extract until smooth and creamy.
3. In a small bowl, using an electric mixer, whip egg white substitute with cream of tartar until it forms stiff peaks.
4. Gently fold whipped egg whites into cream cheese mixture.
5. Coat a 8-inch square cake pan with cooking spray and pour in batter. Place cake pan into a baking pan and pour hot water into baking pan until it reaches halfway up the sides of the cake pan. Place in oven and bake for 30 minutes.
6. Let cool, then refrigerate for at least 4 hours.

▷ **HINT:** You can serve this cheesecake alone or topped with our Raspberry Sauce or Pineapple Salsa (see pages 179 and 177).

MAKES 8 SERVINGS

SERVING GUIDELINES

▶ **FOR LAP-BAND:**
  Weeks 1+: Serve ½ slice of cheesecake.

▶ **FOR BYPASS:**
  Weeks 1+: Serve ½ slice of cheesecake.

▶ **FOR BPD-DS:**
  Week 1+: Serve ½–1 slice cheesecake

▶ **FOR OTHERS:**
  Serve 1 slice of cheesecake.

Calories: 59.13, **Protein:** 7.98g, **Fat:** 0.84g, **Carbohydrates:** 3.91g, **Cholesterol:** 5mg, **Fiber:** 0.34g, **Sodium:** 185.46mg

Minted Cheesecake
with Strawberry Sauce

THIS CHEESECAKE TASTES LIKE SUMMER, THANKS TO THE FRESH MINT LEAVES.

6 ounces fat-free cream cheese,
  softened
½ cup fat-free ricotta cheese
¼ cup fresh mint leaves
5 packets artificial sweetener
  (Splenda or Sweet 'N Low)
¼ teaspoon vanilla extract

Strawberry Sauce
  (makes approximately 1 cup):
1 cup fresh strawberries, sliced
½ cup water
6 packets artificial sweetener
  (Splenda or Sweet 'N Low)
½ teaspoon balsamic vinegar

1. Combine all cheesecake ingredients in food processor and puree until smooth.
2. Pour into four 4-ounce ramekins, cover with plastic wrap, and chill in refrigerator for at least 4 hours.
3. In a small saucepan, combine sauce ingredients and bring to a boil. Reduce heat and simmer for 10 minutes, stirring occasionally, until strawberries are soft and sauce is slightly thickened.
4. Pour into a container, cover, and chill for at least 4 hours.

MAKES 4 SERVINGS

SERVING GUIDELINES

▶ **FOR LAP-BAND:**
Weeks 1+: Serve 2 ounces cheesecake with 2 tablespoons sauce.

▶ **FOR BYPASS:**
Weeks 1+: Serve 2 ounces cheesecake with 2 tablespoons sauce.

▶ **FOR BPD-DS:**
Weeks 1+: Serve 2–4 ounces cheesecake with 2 tablespoons sauce.

▶ **FOR OTHERS:**
Serve 4 ounces cheesecake with sauce.

CHEESECAKE:
  Calories: 75.68, **Protein:** 10.57g, **Fat:** 0.14g, **Carbohydrates:** 8.41g, **Cholesterol:** 10.50mg, **Fiber:** 1.13g, **Sodium:** 229.42mg

**STRAWBERRY SAUCE
(2 TABLESPOONS):**
  Calories: 6.59, **Protein:** 0.13g, **Fat:** 0.08g, **Carbohydrates:** 2.29g, **Cholesterol:** 0mg, **Fiber:** 0.48g, **Sodium:** 5mg

Strawberry Ricotta Whip

THIS LIGHT, FROTHY RECIPE IS TANGY, CREAMY, AND FULL OF FRESH FRUIT FLAVOR.

2½ cups fresh strawberries,
    quartered
½ cup fat-free ricotta cheese
½ cup plain, fat-free yogurt
½ teaspoon grated orange zest
½ teaspoon vanilla extract
4 packets artificial sweetener
6 tablespoons egg white substitute
½ teaspoon cream of tartar

1. Combine strawberries, ricotta, yogurt, orange zest, vanilla, and sweetener in the container of a food processor and process until smooth.
2. In a medium bowl, whip egg white substitute and cream of tartar until stiff peaks form.
3. Gently fold beaten egg whites into strawberry mixture. Pour into 4 small dessert bowls and chill overnight.

MAKES 4 SERVINGS

SERVING GUIDELINES

▶ FOR LAP-BAND:
   Weeks 1+: Serve 2 ounces as is.

▶ FOR BYPASS:
   Weeks 1+: Serve 2 ounces as is.

▶ FOR BPD-DS:
   Weeks 1+: Serve 2–4 ounces as is.

▶ FOR OTHERS:
   Serve 4 ounces as is.

Calories: 85.92, **Protein:** 8.89g, **Fat:** 0.38g, **Carbohydrates:** 14.01g, **Cholesterol:** 3.83mg, **Fiber:** 2.41g, **Sodium:** 85.27mg

Flan

SOME CALL IT FLAN, SOME CALL IT CUSTARD—I CALL IT DELICIOUS. THIS LIGHT, LOW-FAT VERSION IS SURPRISINGLY SATISFYING TO YOUR SWEET TOOTH.

1 12-ounce can of fat-free evaporated milk
½ teaspoon vanilla
8 packets artificial sweetener (Splenda or Sweet 'N Low)
1 large egg plus
1 large egg yolk

Special equipment:
You'll need 6 4-ounce custard cups or ramekins for this recipe.

1. Preheat oven to 350°F.
2. Whisk together all ingredients until smooth.
3. Divide mixture among cups and place cups in a baking pan filled with 1 inch of hot water. Cover baking pan loosely with a sheet of aluminum foil and bake in middle of oven until flan is set but still trembles slightly, 35–40 minutes.
4. Remove cups from baking dish and cool on rack. Then place cups in refrigerator and chill, uncovered, at least 2 hours.
5. Serve in cups or unmold by running a knife around edges to loosen and invert onto plates.

▷ **HINT:** This can be served plain or topped with 2 tablespoons of Papaya Sauce (page 181), Chocolate Sauce (page 178), or Raspberry Sauce (page 179).

MAKES 6 SERVINGS

SERVING GUIDELINES

▶ **FOR LAP-BAND:**
Weeks 1+: Serve 2 ounces as is.

▶ **FOR BYPASS:**
Weeks 1+: Serve 2 ounces as is.

▶ **FOR BPD-DS:**
Weeks 1+: Serve 2–4 ounces as is.

▶ **FOR OTHERS:**
Serve 4 ounces as is.

Calories: 73.33, **Protein:** 5.51g, **Fat:** 1.69g, **Carbohydrates:** 9.53g, **Cholesterol:** 70.86mg, **Fiber:** 0g, **Sodium:** 91.72mg

Lemon Soufflé

THIS TART, FROTHY DESSERT IS REALLY QUITE SIMPLE TO MAKE. THE SECRET IS NOT TO OPEN THE OVEN WHILE IT'S BAKING AND TO SERVE IT IMMEDIATELY.

2 large eggs, separated
¼ cup lemon juice
2 tablespoons lemon zest
6 packets artificial sweetener (Splenda or Sweet 'N Low)
1 12-ounce can fat-free evaporated milk

1. Preheat oven to 350°F.
2. Beat egg whites until stiff.
3. In a separate bowl, mix all other ingredients together and gently fold in egg whites.
4. Pour into a 2-quart casserole or soufflé dish and place dish in a baking pan. Pour hot water into baking pan until it reaches halfway up sides of soufflé dish.
5. Bake for 35 minutes.

MAKES 4 SERVINGS

SERVING GUIDELINES

▶ **FOR LAP-BAND:**
   Weeks 1+: Serve 2 ounces as is.

▶ **FOR BYPASS:**
   Weeks 1+: Serve 2 ounces as is.

▶ **FOR BPD-DS:**
   Weeks 1+: Serve 2–4 ounces as is.

▶ **FOR OTHERS:**
   Serve 4 ounces as is.

Calories: 117.47, **Protein:** 9.23g, **Fat:** 2.51g, **Carbohydrates:** 15.61g, **Cholesterol:** 106.25mg, **Fiber:** 0.38g, **Sodium:** 151.83mg

Apricot and Strawberry Smoothie

IF YOU'RE LOOKING FOR A HEALTHY, PROTEIN-RICH SNACK, FRUIT SMOOTHIES ARE PERFECT. THIS ONE IS FRESH AND TANGY-TASTING, AND THE COLOR IS SPECTACULAR.

*1 small very ripe apricot, pitted
and cut into eighths*
*¼ cup (2) fresh strawberries,
hulled and cut into quarters*
½ cup plain, fat-free yogurt
¼ cup skim milk
1 packet artificial sweetener

SERVING GUIDELINES

▶ FOR EVERYONE:
Serve as is.

1. Place all ingredients in a blender and puree until frothy.

MAKES 1 SERVING

▷ **VARIATION:** Summer slushy—if your blender can crush ice, add 2 ice cubes before blending.

Calories: 137.35, **Protein:** 10.83g, **Fat:** 0.40, **Carbohydrates:** 23.44g, **Cholesterol:** 4.56mg, **Fiber:** 1.79g, **Sodium:** 159.29mg

Minted Summer Smoothie

CUCUMBER IN A SMOOTHIE? YOU'LL BE AMAZED AT HOW REFRESHING IT IS. WE COMBINED IT WITH SWEET MELON, BUT YOU CAN TRY OTHER RIPE FRUIT.

*½ cup ripe honeydew melon,
diced*
*¼ cup cucumber, peeled,
seeded, and diced*
6 fresh mint leaves
½ cup plain, fat-free yogurt
1 packet artificial sweetener
2 ice cubes

SERVING GUIDELINES

▶ FOR EVERYONE:
Serve as is.

1. Put all ingredients in a blender and puree until smooth.
2. Add ice cubes and blend on high speed about 30 seconds until chilled.

MAKES 1 SERVING

Calories: 140.25, **Protein:** 9.71g, **Fat:** 0.42g, **Carbohydrates:** 26.55g, **Cholesterol:** 3.33mg, **Fiber:** 3.01g, **Sodium:** 144.62mg

Piña Colada Smoothie

TALK ABOUT TROPICAL—THIS SMOOTHIE BRINGS BACK MEMORIES OF ISLAND BEACHES, HIBIS-
CUS FLOWERS, AND SOFT BREEZES. IN OTHER WORDS, YOU'LL HAVE A VACATION IN A GLASS.

½ cup plain, fat-free yogurt
¼ cup fresh pineapple, diced
¼ cup fresh mango, diced
2 packets artificial sweetener
½ teaspoon coconut extract
3 ice cubes

1. Place all ingredients in a blender and puree until
   frothy.

SERVES 1

SERVING GUIDELINES

▶ FOR EVERYONE:
Serve as is.

Calories: 132.47, **Protein:** 8.36g, **Fat:** 0.28g, **Carbohydrates:** 26.48g,
Cholesterol: 3.33mg, **Fiber:** 1.21g, **Sodium:** 127.88mg

Hot Chocolate

SURPRISE, SURPRISE—HOT CHOCOLATE IS ALLOWABLE, AS LONG AS IT'S MADE LIKE THIS.
ACTUALLY, IT'S A GREAT WAY TO GET YOUR DAILY PROTEIN AND CALCIUM.

1 tablespoon unsweetened
   cocoa
1 packet artificial sweetener
   (Splenda or Sweet 'N Low)
1 cup skim milk

1. Mix cocoa and sweetener in cup or mug.
2. Add ¼ cup milk and stir to make a paste.
3. Heat remaining milk in microwave for 45 seconds to
   1 minute or until hot, and add hot milk to cocoa mixture, stirring until smooth.

MAKES 1 SERVING

▷ **VARIATIONS:** Add ⅛ teaspoon cinnamon, ½ teaspoon
   instant decaf coffee, ⅛ teaspoon vanilla, or ⅛ teaspoon coconut extract.
▷ **HINT:** In the summer, if your blender can crush ice, you
   can make frozen hot cocoa: let hot cocoa cool, then
   put in blender with 1 ice cube and blend until frothy.

SERVING GUIDELINES

▶ FOR EVERYONE:
Serve as is.

Calories: 98.11, **Protein:** 9.40g,
Fat: 1.19g, **Carbohydrates:** 15.82g,
Cholesterol: 4.90mg, **Fiber:** 1.80g,
Sodium: 128.54mg

Savory & Sweet Sauces

Wait a minute. Can you really eat sauces? Aren't you trying to lose weight? The answer is yes to both. All these sauce recipes are low in calories and carbs and have no added sugars. What they do have is lots of flavor.

Sauces are very important for two reasons: First, during your early post-operative period, you'll need some kind of liquid base to make a smooth puree, and these sauces work perfectly and taste amazing. Second, if you try to lose weight by eating nothing but dry broiled and baked food for the rest of your life, you'll be miserable and probably cheat or just give up. With these delicious sauces, you can eat right and enjoy every mouthful.

In this section you'll find both savory and sweet sauces. A savory sauce can be a creamy sauce with a horseradish punch or a mixture of chopped vegetables with wine and broth; a quick, light tomato sauce; a spicy salsa; or a tangy mixture of fresh plums, tomato paste, and spices. Our sweet sauces include a surprisingly luscious chocolate sauce, but you'll also discover fresh fruit sauces that are versatile enough to top one of our low-fat desserts, perk up a plain piece of chicken or fish, or stir into yogurt (plain, fat-free yogurt, of course).

So, sauce it up and enjoy your meals even more. With our sauces there's no reason not to.

Note: The nutritional analyses are based on a two-tablespoon serving.

Versatile entrée and dessert sauces layer on taste and texture

Asian Dipping Sauce

THIS IS OUR VERSION OF THE CLASSIC SAUCE THAT'S OFTEN SERVED WITH DUMPLINGS AND OTHER CHINESE APPETIZERS.

¾ cup light soy sauce
¼ cup rice vinegar
2 teaspoons red pepper flakes
   or to taste
1 teaspoon sesame oil
brown-sugar artificial sweetener (equivalent of 1 teaspoon)

Calories: 14.77, **Protein:** 1.25g,
Fat: 0.36g, **Carbohydrates:** 1.74g,
Cholesterol: 0mg, **Fiber:** 0.06g,
Sodium: 406.57mg

1. In a small bowl, combine all ingredients and mix well.
2. Cover and refrigerate for 10–20 minutes to let flavors blend before serving.

MAKES APPROXIMATELY 1 CUP

▷ **HINT:** This sauce can be refrigerated for up to one week. It also makes a great liquid base for purees.
▷ **SERVING SUGGESTIONS:** Try it with our Asian Turkey Filled Dumplings (page 88) or Singapore Shrimp Dumplings (page 142). It's also tasty with simple broiled chicken or fish.

Caesar Sauce

THIS IS A LOW-FAT VERSION OF THE CLASSIC CAESAR DRESSING. BUT WHY JUST STOP AT SALADS? IT'S A TASTY ADDITION TO LOTS OF DISHES.

¼ cup Dijon mustard
¼ cup grated Parmesan cheese
4 cloves garlic, minced
2 tablespoons anchovy paste
2 tablespoons Worcestershire
   sauce
¼ cup balsamic vinegar
¼ cup plain, fat-free yogurt

Calories: 24.79, **Protein:** 1.41g,
Fat: 1.23g, **Carbohydrates:** 2.78g,
Cholesterol: 8.58mg, **Fiber:** 0.08g,
Sodium: 230.18mg

1. Combine all ingredients in a blender or food processor and puree until smooth.

MAKES APPROXIMATELY 1 CUP

▷ **HINT:** This sauce makes a great liquid base for purees.
▷ **SERVING SUGGESTIONS:** This sauce is extremely versatile—you can try it on fish or chicken, use as a salad dressing, toss with cooked green vegetables (serve hot or cold), and even add some prepared horseradish and serve with cold beef or veal.

Garlic Sauce

THIS PUNGENT SAUCE IS A DELICIOUS WAY TO ENHANCE THE FLAVOR OF SIMPLE ROASTED, BROILED, OR POACHED FOODS. YOU CAN SERVE IT HOT OR COLD.

½ cup plain, fat-free yogurt
4 garlic cloves, finely minced
1 tablespoon fresh lemon juice
½ cup chicken broth

1. Pour yogurt into a fine mesh strainer over a small bowl and let stand for 15 minutes. Discard any liquid that has drained from yogurt.
2. In a small bowl, crush garlic until it forms a paste and stir in lemon juice.
3. Add drained yogurt to garlic mixture and stir well.
4. In small saucepan, bring chicken broth to a simmer, stir in yogurt-garlic mixture, and simmer for 1 minute more, stirring constantly.

MAKES APPROXIMATELY 1 CUP

▷ **HINT:** This sauce makes a great liquid base for purees.
▷ **SERVING SUGGESTIONS:** A perfect topping for beef, lamb, chicken, turkey loaf—even poached fish.

Calories: 7.12, **Protein:** 0.59g, **Fat:** 0.01g, **Carbohydrates:** 1.19g, **Cholesterol:** 0.21mg, **Fiber:** 0.02g, **Sodium:** 29.43mg

Spicy-Creamy Citrus Sauce

THIS CREAMY SAUCE IS A FUSION OF ASIAN AND CUBAN FLAVORS—COOL, YET HOT.

½ cup fat-free sour cream

2 tablespoons low-sodium soy sauce

2 tablespoon freshly squeezed lime juice

2 tablespoon freshly squeezed orange juice

brown-sugar artificial sweetener (½ teaspoon equivalent)

½ teaspoon Asian chili paste with garlic

1 tablespoon finely grated fresh ginger

¼ cup chopped fresh basil

1. In a small bowl, combine all ingredients and mix well. If not using right away, refrigerate. Sauce can be refrigerated in a tightly sealed container up to 1 week.

2. Bring sauce to room temperature when ready to serve.

MAKES APPROXIMATELY 1 CUP

▷ **SERVING SUGGESTIONS:** This sauce tastes excellent on baked or broiled shrimp, salmon, swordfish, or tuna. You can also use it as a dipping sauce for shrimp cocktail.

Calories: 13.62, **Protein:** 0.74g, **Fat:** 0.01g, **Carbohydrates:** 2.19g, **Cholesterol:** 1.25mg, **Fiber:** 0.07g, **Sodium:** 76.18mg

Citrus-Horseradish Sauce

THIS CREAMY TOPPING GETS ITS HEAT FROM HORSERADISH AND ITS COOL FRESHNESS FROM CITRUS. IT'S A QUICK UNCOOKED SAUCE THAT CAN LIVEN UP LOTS OF DISHES.

½ cup fat-free sour cream
½ cup low-fat mayonnaise
1 tablespoon fresh lemon juice
1 tablespoon fresh lime juice
1 teaspoon lemon zest, finely grated
1 teaspoon lime zest, finely grated
2 teaspoons capers
2 teaspoons bottled white horse-radish
½ cup fresh basil leaves, chopped

1. Combine all ingredients in a small bowl and whisk until smooth.

MAKES APPROXIMATELY 1 CUP

▷ **HINT:** This sauce makes a great liquid base for purees.
▷ **SERVING SUGGESTIONS:** This is delicious as a sauce for fish, chicken, pork, or beef. You can also use it as a base for tuna, egg, or salmon salad, and it works well as a salad dressing or tossed with cold or hot cooked vegetables.

Calories: 35.48, **Protein:** 0.67g, **Fat:** 2.64g, **Carbohydrates:** 2.39g, **Cholesterol:** 3.75mg, **Fiber:** 0.09g, **Sodium:** 83.84mg

Creamy Basil-Seafood Sauce

THIS SAUCE PACKS A POWERFUL PUNCH, SO YOU JUST NEED TO USE A LITTLE BIT. IT MAKES A TERRIFIC GLAZE AS WELL AS A SAUCE FOR BROILED OR BAKED FISH.

½ cup fat-free sour cream
½ cup low-fat mayonnaise
2 tablespoons prepared horse-radish
¼ cup fresh basil, chopped
2 teaspoons light soy sauce
2 tablespoons minced onion
1 teaspoon fresh ginger, minced
1 tablespoon anchovy paste

1. Combine all ingredients in a medium bowl and mix well.

MAKES APPROXIMATELY 1 CUP

▷ **HINT:** This sauce makes a great liquid base for purees.
▷ **SERVING SUGGESTIONS:** This sauce gives you a tangy way to perk up poached or broiled fish. You can also mix it into tuna or salmon salad instead of mayonnaise or use it as a dip for vegetables or cold steamed shrimp.

Calories: 38.86, **Protein:** 1.10g, **Fat:** 3.04g, **Carbohydrates:** 2.60g, **Cholesterol:** 7.19mg, **Fiber:** 0.05g, **Sodium:** 165.77mg

Shallot-Horseradish Sauce

Creamy with a bit of a kick, this lovely pale-pink sauce dresses up even the simplest of entrées.

cooking spray
¼ cup shallots, minced
1½ teaspoons garlic, minced
¼ cup white wine
1 tablespoon condensed chicken broth
¾ cup plain, fat-free yogurt
1 teaspoon sweet paprika
1 tablespoon prepared horse-radish

1. Coat a small nonstick saucepan with cooking spray and sauté shallots and garlic over medium-high heat until soft but not browned.
2. Add white wine and condensed chicken broth, reduce heat, and bring to a slow simmer.
3. Add yogurt, paprika, and horseradish and cook, barely simmering, for 5 minutes until slightly reduced.

MAKES APPROXIMATELY 1 CUP

▷ **HINT:** This sauce makes a great liquid base for purees.
▷ **SERVING SUGGESTIONS:** This makes a tangy addition to broiled or sautéed chicken, turkey, or pork. You can also serve cold with beef or lamb.

Calories: 15.45, **Protein:** 1.04g, **Fat:** 0.25g, **Carbohydrates:** 2.08g, **Cholesterol:** 0.31mg, **Fiber:** 0.03g, **Sodium:** 79.03mg

Simple Horseradish Sauce

It couldn't be easier—no cutting, no chopping, no cooking—just a piquant, bold taste that adds a kick to even the most basic dishes.

1 cup fat-free sour cream
3 tablespoons concentrated chicken broth
2 teaspoons sweet paprika
2 tablespoons prepared horse-radish

1. In a small bowl, combine all ingredients and mix well. If not using right away, refrigerate. Sauce can be refrigerated in a tightly sealed container up to 1 week.
2. Bring sauce to room temperature when ready to serve.

MAKES APPROXIMATELY 1 CUP

▷ **SERVING SUGGESTIONS:** Use to top off our Turkey Loaf (page 92). This sauce is also great on broiled chicken, sautéed chicken, or turkey cutlets and can really sauce up a turkey burger.

Calories: 24.09, **Protein:** 1.41g, **Fat:** 0.54g, **Carbohydrates:** 3.79g, **Cholesterol:** 54mg, **Fiber:** 0.05g, **Sodium:** 202mg

Creamy Wasabi Sauce

Adding Asian ingredients to a creamy base makes this unusual sauce delicious as well as very versatile.

½ cup fat-free sour cream
½ cup low-fat mayonnaise
1 tablespoon light soy sauce
1 packet artificial sweetener
2 teaspoons wasabi paste

1. Mix all ingredients together in a small bowl until well blended.

MAKES APPROXIMATELY 1 CUP

▷ **HINT:** This sauce makes a great liquid base for purees.
▷ **SERVING SUGGESTIONS:** Use this sauce to add just a hint of heat to fish and shrimp, try it as a dip with raw vegetables, or mix it into tuna, chicken, or salmon salad instead of plain mayonnaise.

Calories: 36.59, **Protein:** 0.60g, **Fat:** 2.56g, **Carbohydrates:** 2.57g, **Cholesterol:** 3.75mg, **Fiber:** 0g, **Sodium:** 110.13mg

Quick Tomato Sauce

FOR YEARS I'VE MADE MY OWN SLOW-COOKED TOMATO SAUCE WITH FRESH PLUM TOMA-
TOES. BUT WHEN FRESH TOMATOES ARE NOT IN SEASON, OR WHEN I JUST DON'T HAVE THE
TIME, I MAKE THIS LIGHT, SIMPLE VERSION.

olive oil cooking spray
1 clove garlic, minced
1 14.5-ounce can diced toma-
toes
1 packet artificial sweetener
(Splenda or Sweet 'N Low)
2 tablespoons fresh basil leaves,
chopped

1. In a medium nonstick saucepan, heat cooking spray, add garlic, and sauté until slightly browned.
2. Add tomatoes, sweetener, and basil, turn down heat, and simmer for 5–7 minutes.

MAKES APPROXIMATELY 1 CUP

▷ **HINT:** This sauce makes a great liquid base for purees.
▷ **SERVING SUGGESTIONS:** This topping gives a light, Italian accent to fish, chicken, meatloaf, turkey loaf, or meatballs. You can also spoon it on sautéed or broiled sliced steak.

Calories: 8.79, **Protein:** 0.44g, **Fat:** 0g, **Carbohydrates:** 1.82g, **Cholesterol:** 0mg, **Fiber:** 0.44g, **Sodium:** 40.06mg

Sauce Piperade

THIS IS SIMILAR TO OUR SAUCE BASQUAISE BUT WITHOUT THE WINE AND BEEF BROTH, JUST LOTS OF LOVELY FRESH VEGETABLES AND GARLIC.

olive oil cooking spray
¼ cup onion, chopped
1 clove garlic, chopped
¼ cup green bell pepper, diced
¼ cup red bell pepper, diced
¼ pound white mushrooms, sliced
¼ cup plum tomatoes, seeded and chopped
salt and freshly ground pepper to taste

1. Coat a medium nonstick skillet with cooking spray. Over a medium-high flame, sauté onion and garlic until lightly browned.
2. Lower flame to medium, add peppers and mushrooms to pan, and cook, covered, for 3–5 minutes until soft.
3. Add tomatoes and cook, stirring occasionally, for 2 minutes until tomatoes have softened and sauce has thickened.

MAKES APPROXIMATELY 1 CUP

▷ **HINT:** This sauce makes a great liquid base for purees.
▷ **SERVING SUGGESTIONS:** Try stirring this sauce into scrambled eggs or folding into an omelet. It's also delicious with any kind of fish or seafood and terrific for topping a chicken or turkey cutlet.

Calories: 4.80, **Protein:** 0.32g, **Fat:** 0.06g, **Carbohydrates:** 0.98g, **Cholesterol:** 0mg, **Fiber:** 0.26g, **Sodium:** 1.05mg

Sauce Basquaise

THIS STARTED OUT AS A TRADITIONAL BASQUE SAUCE—PEPPERS, TOMATOES, AND ONIONS—THEN WE ADDED LOTS OF OTHER GOOD STUFF.

olive oil cooking spray
¼ cup chopped onion
1 clove garlic, chopped
¼ cup green bell pepper, diced
¼ cup red bell pepper, diced
¼ pound white mushrooms, sliced
¼ cup red wine
¼ cup plum tomatoes, seeded and chopped
1½ teaspoons concentrated beef broth
salt and freshly ground pepper to taste

1. Coat a medium nonstick skillet with cooking spray and sauté onions and garlic over a medium-high flame until lightly browned.
2. Lower flame to medium; add peppers and mushrooms to pan and cook, covered, for 3–5 minutes until soft.
3. Add wine, tomatoes, and beef broth concentrate and cook, stirring occasionally, for 3 minutes until sauce has thickened and reduced by half.

MAKES APPROXIMATELY 1 CUP

▷ **HINT:** This sauce makes a great liquid base for purees.
▷ **SERVING SUGGESTIONS:** This sauce is excellent with beef (steak, London broil, meatloaf, burgers, or meatballs) and also works well with lamb or veal.

Calories: 10.81, **Protein:** 0.43g, **Fat:** 0.06g, **Carbohydrates:** 1.15g, **Cholesterol:** 0mg, **Fiber:** 0.26g, **Sodium:** 44.54mg

Yogurt-Mint Sauce

THIS SAUCE REPRESENTS A CLASSIC GREEK BLEND OF FLAVORS—COOL AND MINTY, WITH THE TANGINESS OF LEMON AND YOGURT.

¾ cup plain, fat-free yogurt
1 small garlic clove, quartered
1 teaspoon cumin
½ teaspoon lemon zest
1 tablespoon fresh lemon juice
½ cup mint leaves
2 teaspoons chicken broth concentrate

1. Place all ingredients in a food processor and puree until smooth.

MAKES APPROXIMATELY 1 CUP

▷ **HINT:** This sauce makes a great liquid base for purees.
▷ **SERVING SUGGESTIONS:** This Mediterranean way to spark up lamb and swordfish also makes a good salad dressing. Try mixing it with cooked vegetables or using it as a dip for crudités.

Calories: 15.25, **Protein:** 1.08g, **Fat:** 0.13g, **Carbohydrates:** 2.52g, **Cholesterol:** 0.31mg, **Fiber:** 0.63g, **Sodium:** 51.92mg

Tikka Yogurt Sauce

This classic Indian sauce blends a complex mix of spices into a taste–bud tingling experience.

cooking spray
1 tablespoon garlic, minced
¾ cup yogurt
¼ cup low-sodium, low-fat chicken broth
½ small red chili, seeded and minced
½ teaspoon cumin
½ teaspoon ground coriander
½ teaspoon turmeric
½ teaspoon garam masala
2 tablespoons lime juice
salt and pepper to taste

1. Coat a small saucepan with cooking spray and sauté garlic until soft.
2. Add all other ingredients and cook over low heat for 3 minutes.

Makes approximately 1 cup

▷ **HINT:** This sauce makes a great liquid base for purees.
▷ **SERVING SUGGESTIONS:** This sauce gives an Indian accent to fish and chicken dishes. It also makes a great salad dressing, or can be mixed with cooked vegetables, served hot or cold.

Calories: 10.77, **Protein:** 0.85g, **Fat:** 0.04g, **Carbohydrates:** 1.75g, **Cholesterol:** 0.31mg, **Fiber:** 0.11g, **Sodium:** 22.91mg

Sweet-and-Sour Sauce

IF YOU HAVE OR HAD A GRANDMA FROM ONE OF THE MIDDLE EUROPEAN COUNTRIES OR RUSSIA, YOU PROBABLY REMEMBER HER SAVORY SWEET-AND-SOUR RECIPES. WITH THAT TASTE MEMORY AS A GUIDELINE, WE CREATED THIS LIGHTER, MORE CITRUSY VERSION.

cooking spray
¼ cup onion, minced
1½ teaspoons fresh ginger,
  minced
1½ teaspoons tomato paste
1 8-ounce can tomato sauce
  (no salt added)
2 tablespoons orange juice
1½ teaspoons red wine vinegar
1 packet artificial sweetener
  (Splenda or Sweet 'N Low)

1. In a large nonstick skillet, heat cooking spray until hot but not smoking.
2. Sauté onion until just soft but not brown. Add ginger and stir for 30 seconds. Add all other sauce ingredients and simmer for 5 minutes.

MAKES APPROXIMATELY 1 CUP

▷ **HINT:** This sauce makes a great liquid base for purees.
▷ **SERVING SUGGESTIONS:** You can use this as the sauce for our Sweet-and-Sour Stuffed Cabbage (page 87) or try it as a topping on broiled halibut or swordfish. It's delicious with our Turkey Loaf (page 92) or mixed with beef or turkey meatballs, and it also tastes great on poached or broiled chicken.

Calories: 7.70, **Protein:** 0.30g, **Fat:** 0g, **Carbohydrates:** 1.74g, **Cholesterol:** 0mg, **Fiber:** 0.29g, **Sodium:** 7.28mg

Fresh Plum Sauce

This is one of those extremely versatile recipes that I just adore. It adds another dimension of flavor to a wide variety of foods—from Asian recipes to Indian curries, and even to good old American comfort food.

cooking spray
½ cup onion, chopped
3 large red or purple plums,
   seeded and chopped
1 clove garlic, minced
1 tablespoon tomato paste
½ small jalapeño pepper,
   seeded and minced
1 tablespoon balsamic vinegar
1 tablespoon light soy sauce
brown-sugar artificial sweetener
   (1 teaspoon equivalent)

1. Coat a nonstick saucepan with cooking spray, heat, and sauté onion until just translucent.
2. Add all other ingredients and cook over low flame for 10 minutes until thick.
3. Let cool slightly, pour into a food processor, and blend until smooth.

Makes approximately 1 cup

▷ **HINT:** This sauce makes a great liquid base for purees.
▷ **SERVING SUGGESTIONS:** This sauce adds a tangy note to pork, poultry, and shrimp. You can also use it as a cooking glaze or a dipping sauce. I often use it in place of hoisin sauce. Thin it out with a little more soy and vinegar and use it as a marinade. Serve it as a condiment with Indian or Pakistani curries. It also makes a great substitute for ketchup (much lower in sugar) on meatloaf, or mixed into your meatloaf recipe (2 tablespoons) before cooking.

Calories: 12.11, **Protein:** 0.34g, **Fat:** 0.09g, **Carbohydrates:** 2.70g, **Cholesterol:** 0mg, **Fiber:** 0.32g, **Sodium:** 49.06mg

Mango Salsa

I LOVE FRUIT SAUCES, ESPECIALLY SAVORY SALSAS, LIKE THIS ONE, THAT CONTRAST THE SWEETNESS OF FRESH TROPICAL FRUIT WITH THE HEAT OF CHILI. OF COURSE, IF YOU REALLY LIKE IT HOT, INCREASE THE CHILI POWDER OR ADD A WHOLE MINCED HOT PEPPER.

¼ cup chicken broth
¾ cup fresh, ripe mango, diced
⅓ cup red onion, sliced thin
1 tablespoon balsamic vinegar
½ packet artificial sweetener
  (Splenda or Sweet 'N Low)
1 teaspoon chili powder

1. In a small saucepan, bring chicken broth to a slow boil.
2. Add all other ingredients and cook about 10 minutes until thick.
3. Puree for a smooth sauce, or serve chunky.

MAKES APPROXIMATELY 1 CUP

▷ **HINT:** This sauce makes a great liquid base for purees. Can be refrigerated, tightly sealed, for up to 2 weeks.
▷ **SERVING SUGGESTIONS:** Use this sauce to really zing up regular or smoked pork chops, chicken, or stronger-flavored fish such as fresh salmon, tuna, swordfish, or shrimp. It also makes a delicious dip.

Calories: 7.69, **Protein:** 0.10g, **Fat:** 0.05g, **Carbohydrates:** 1.92g, **Cholesterol:** 0mg, **Fiber:** 0.24g, **Sodium:** 26.87mg

Papaya Salsa

COMBINING THE MELLOW SWEETNESS OF PAPAYA WITH THE HOT KICK OF CHILI POWDER IS A VERY TROPICAL TRADITION.

¼ cup chicken broth
¾ cup fresh, very ripe papaya, diced
⅓ cup red onion, sliced thin
1 tablespoon balsamic vinegar
½ packet artificial sweetener (Splenda or Sweet 'N Low)
1 teaspoon chili powder

1. In a small saucepan, bring chicken broth to a slow boil.
2. Add all other ingredients and cook about 10 minutes until thick.
3. Puree for a smooth sauce or serve chunky.

MAKES APPROXIMATELY 1 CUP

▷ **HINT:** This sauce makes a great liquid base for purees.
▷ **SERVING SUGGESTIONS:** This sauce adds some spark to regular or smoked pork chops, chicken, or stronger-flavored fish such as fresh salmon, tuna, swordfish, or shrimp. It also makes a tasty dip.

Calories: 5.23, **Protein:** 0.10g, **Fat:** 0.04g, **Carbohydrates:** 1.25g, **Cholesterol:** 0mg, **Fiber:** 0.21g, **Sodium:** 26.91mg

Pineapple Salsa

THERE'S NOTHING BETTER THAN THE SWEET JUICINESS OF A FRESH PINEAPPLE, EXCEPT
MAYBE THIS FRESH PINEAPPLE SALSA.

1 cup fresh pineapple, cut up
3 tablespoons orange juice
1½ teaspoons red-wine vinegar
1 teaspoon red chili paste
1 teaspoon garlic, finely
* minced*
¼ teaspoon sesame oil
brown-sugar artificial sweetener
* (1 teaspoon equivalent)*

1. Combine all ingredients in a food processor and pulse
   till coarsely blended.

MAKES APPROXIMATELY 1 CUP

▷ **HINT:** This sauce makes a great liquid base for purees.
▷ **SERVING SUGGESTIONS:** This is a classic salsa that really
livens up meat, poultry, shrimp, or fish. You can also
use it as a dip.

Calories: 7.18, **Protein:** 0.06g, **Fat:** 0.12g, **Carbohydrates:** 1.60g,
Cholesterol: 0mg, **Fiber:** 0.14g, **Sodium:** 1.58mg

Chocolate Sauce

We couldn't believe it when we created this thick, rich-tasting sauce that has virtually no fat. It's real chocolate sauce, no kidding.

1 cup evaporated skim milk

8 tablespoons unsweetened cocoa

6 packets artificial sweetener (Splenda or Sweet 'N Low)

1. In a small saucepan, bring evaporated milk to a simmer.
2. Pour ¼ cup milk into a small bowl and stir in cocoa until it forms a smooth paste.
3. Simmer rest of milk for 2–3 minutes to reduce and thicken slightly.
4. Add cocoa paste and sweetener to milk in sauce pan and stir over low heat until smooth.
5. Chill, covered, in refrigerator for at least 1 hour (if too thick, stir in a little more evaporated milk until it reaches desired consistency).
6. Can be served hot, like hot fudge sauce, or at room temperature.

Makes approximately 1 cup

▷ **SERVING SUGGESTIONS:** This luscious topping tastes fantastic on the Flan (page 157). You can also try pouring it over water-packed canned or poached fruit or using it as a topping on fat-free, sugar-free ice cream or frozen yogurt.

Calories: 18.68, **Protein:** 1.53g, **Fat:** 0.38g, **Carbohydrates:** 3.85g, **Cholesterol:** 0mg, **Fiber:** 0.90g, **Sodium:** 20.57mg

Raspberry Sauce

THIS IS A BRIGHT, TANGY SAUCE THAT, THANKS TO THE AVAILABILITY OF FRESH-FROZEN RASPBERRIES, TASTES LIKE SUMMER ALL YEAR LONG.

1 cup fresh-frozen raspberries
6 packets artificial sweetener
  (Splenda or Sweet 'N Low)
½ cup water
1 tablespoon lemon juice

1. In a saucepan, mix raspberries, artificial sweetener, water, and lemon juice and bring to a boil, then lower heat and simmer for 10 minutes.
2. Remove from heat; cool and strain through a fine sieve into a bowl, pressing down to catch all liquids. Discard seeds and solids.
3. Cover and chill in refrigerator for 30 minutes.

MAKES APPROXIMATELY 1 CUP

▷ **SERVING SUGGESTIONS:** This classic topping tastes amazing on the Flan (page 157), Basic Cheesecake (page 154), and Lemon Soufflé (page 158) recipes. Try pouring it over water-packed canned or poached fruit and fat-free, sugar-free ice cream or frozen yogurt. You can even mix it into plain, fat-free yogurt.

Calories: 4.01, **Protein:** 0.07g, **Fat:** 0.04g, **Carbohydrates:** 1.35g, **Cholesterol:** 0mg, **Fiber:** 0.53g, **Sodium:** 0.01mg

Strawberry Sauce

WHILE YOU CAN PROBABLY MAKE THIS SAUCE WITH FROZEN STRAWBERRIES, I PREFER TO WAIT FOR REALLY RIPE, FRESH BERRIES.

1 cup fresh strawberries, sliced
½ cup water
6 packets artificial sweetener
   (Splenda or Sweet 'N Low)
½ teaspoon balsamic vinegar

1. In a small saucepan, combine sauce ingredients and bring to a boil. Reduce heat and simmer for 10 minutes, stirring occasionally, until strawberries are soft and sauce is slightly thickened.
2. Pour into a container, cover, and chill for at least 4 hours.

MAKES APPROXIMATELY 1 CUP

▷ **SERVING SUGGESTIONS:** This classic topping tastes great on the Flan (page 157), Basic Cheesecake (page 154), Minted Cheesecake (page 155), Lemon Soufflé (page 158), and Strawberry Ricotta Whip (page 156) recipes. You can also try pouring it over water-packed canned or poached fruit and as a topping on fat-free, sugar-free ice cream or frozen yogurt. You can even mix it into plain, fat-free yogurt.

Calories: 6.59, **Protein:** 0.13g, **Fat:** 0.08g, **Carbohydrates:** 2.29g, **Cholesterol:** 0mg, **Fiber:** 0.48g, **Sodium:** 5mg

Papaya Sauce

HERE'S A PERFECT WAY TO ADD A LIGHT TASTE OF THE TROPICS TO LOW-FAT, LOW-CARB DESSERTS. BUT DON'T STOP AT DESSERTS; THIS IS A VERY VERSATILE SAUCE FOR MAIN DISHES, TOO.

1 cup (½ large) very ripe papaya
¼ teaspoon vanilla extract
1 tablespoon lime juice
artificial sweetener to taste (optional)

1. Peel and seed papaya and scoop flesh into a food processor or blender.
2. Add vanilla and lime juice and puree until very smooth (if the sauce is not sweet enough, add artificial sweetener to taste).

MAKES APPROXIMATELY 1 CUP

▷ **SERVING SUGGESTIONS:** This works wonderfully as either a savory meal sauce or a dessert sauce. Try it with poultry, pork, or shrimp, or use as a topping for the luscious Flan recipe (page 157). Pour over fat-free, sugar-free ice cream or frozen yogurt, or mix into plain, fat-free yogurt.

Calories: 3.86, **Protein:** 0.06g, **Fat:** 0.01g, **Carbohydrates:** 0.95g, **Cholesterol:** 0mg, **Fiber:** 0.16g, **Sodium:** 0.28mg

Acknowledgments

$\mathcal{W}$HILE WE HAVE too many supportive friends and family members to list individually, there are a few who we'd like to especially acknowledge. Thank you to Bob Levine, my adoring and adorable husband of many years, and our primary guinea pig (who, by the way, lost a lot of weight on our eating program). Thank you to Michael Saray, Michele's fabulous husband, partner, and best friend, for his unwavering support and pride in her newest accomplishment. To Elyse Schapira, Michele's sister, for her early advice and assistance. A warm thanks to Dr. Inabnet and Meredith Urban-Skuro, for not only helping me to start a new way of life both physically and emotionally, but for all their enthusiasm and involvement in this book. Thank you to Dr. William Suozzi, the primary care physician for Bob and me, as well as for Michele and Michael, who had the compassion to suggest and discuss the possibility of weight reduction surgery for me. Thank you to Deirdre Mullane, without whom we might never have found our way to Marlowe & Company. And, finally, thank you so much to Matthew Lore, our incredible publisher, who knew from the very beginning what we were talking about and just how to help us accomplish it. And we can't forget Peter Jacoby, Matthew's assistant, for all his invaluable assistance. And finally, thank you, thank you to Suzanne McCloskey, our editor, for all her patience and very smart suggestions.

Thank you all so much.

Index